riverpeople

Also by Peter Lamborn Wilson

From Autonomedia:
Escape From the Nineteenth Century
Shower of Stars: Dream and Book
Pirate Utopias

From City Lights:
Ploughing the Clouds: The Search for Irish Soma
Sacred Drift: Essays on the Margins of Islam

From Station Hill Press:
Ec(o)logues

riverpeople

Peter Lamborn Wilson

Autonomedia

This book is dedicated to all those who helped.
Their names are mentioned in the text.

NYSCA
New York State Council on the Arts

This publication made possible, in part, with funds from
the New York State Council on the Arts, a state agency.

ISBN: 978-1-57027-260-8

Autonomedia
POB 568 Williamsburgh Station
Brooklyn, NY 11211-0568 USA

www.autonomedia.org
info@autonomedia.org

Contents

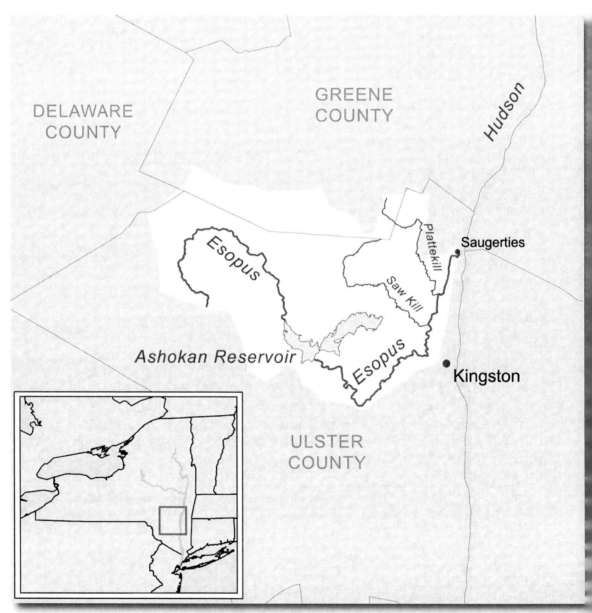

Esopus River, Southern Catskills, New York State

Introduction

The origin of this mixed poetry/prose/text, with geography & history in it, lies in an old ambition of mine to write an epic about every creek river pond swimming hole and large puddle of water in the whole of Ulster County, New York — which I soon gave up in consternation upon realizing that the number of waters might far outnumber the veins nerves & lymph nodes of a human body — a giant human, buried in or identical with the whole County, or even the whole bio-clime, with an almost infinitely complex system of waters, a hydraulic theory-body of endless ramifications & variations, very like a Mandelbrot set — but *written on flowing water.*

So the scope had to be narrowed down to *one* "kill" or creek/river which could be followed, all inside the County, from source to confluence with the Hudson River, the giant tidal fjord that drains & shapes our entire region. Although I've carried out research on several local rivers, such as the beautiful but crippled Rondout with its phantom-double ruined canal, or the somnolent & muddy Wallkill (that flows north like a little Nile), I decided to limit this "epic" to seven historical/geographical/aesthetic events that once took place along the euphoniously-named ESOPUS River, with which I fell in green love, & which was all contained (in a great spiral) within the borders of Ulster.

Already an obsession had arisen concerning the name — first, because of ESOPUS Island (in the Hudson River between Ulster & Dutchess counties); and — second, because of a growing fascination with the Esopus Indians after whom the river and island are named.

In Summer 1918 the poet-magician Aleister Crowley camped out on Esopus Island; according to local legend the Esopus Indians had called it Raphoes and visited it in the spring as a shad fishery. Capt. Kidd supposedly used it as a recruiting base and rendezvous for would-be pirates. There Crowley occupied himself by "translating" the *Tao Te Ching;* investigating his previous incarnations (amongst others he'd been Edward Kelly and Cagliostro); dallying with weekend candidates for the position of Scarlet Woman; and mystifying the locals. In huge red letters he painted his famous motto on a flat rock facing the River: DO WHAT THOU WILT SHALL BE THE WHOLE OF THE LAW. (You can read about Crowley's island idyll in his *Confessions.*)

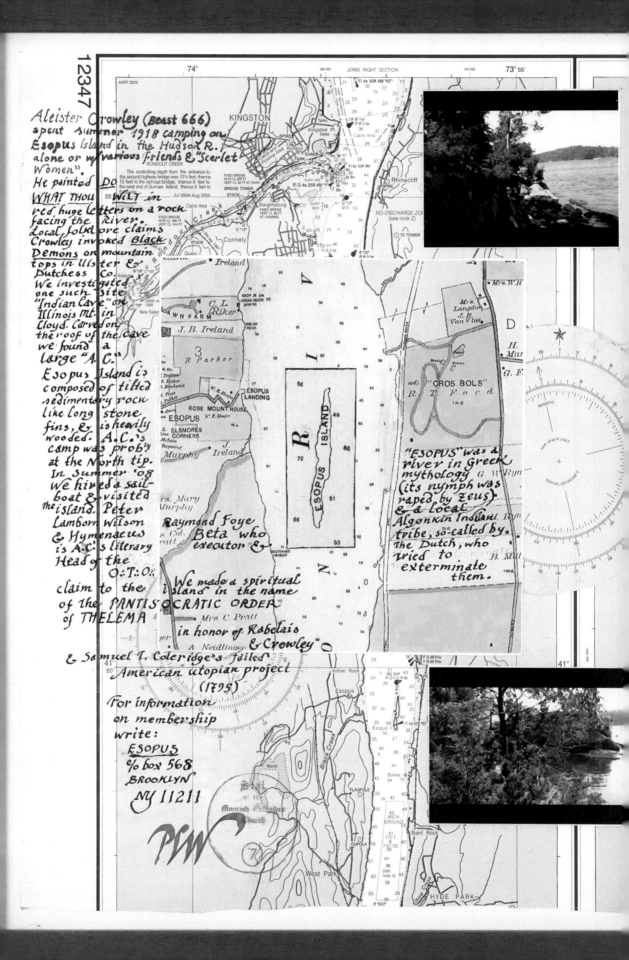

12347

Aleister Crowley (Beast 666) spent summer 1918 camping on Esopus Island in the Hudson R. alone or w/ various friends & "Scarlet Women".

He painted DO WHAT THOU WILT in red, huge letters on a rock facing the River. Local folklore claims Crowley invoked Black Demons on mountain tops in Ulster & Dutchess Co. We investigated one such site "Indian Cave" on Illinois Mt. in Lloyd. Carved on the roof of the cave we found a large "A.C."

Esopus Island is composed of tilted sedimentary rock like long stone fins, & is heavily wooded. A.C.'s camp was prob'y at the North tip. In Summer '08 We hired a sailboat & visited the island. Peter Lamborn Wilson & Hymenaeus is A.C.'s literary Head of the O∴T∴O∴ claim to the of the PANTISOCRATIC ORDER of THELEMA

& Samuel T. Coleridge's failed American utopian project (1795)

For information on membership write:
ESOPUS
c/o box 568
BROOKLYN
NY 11211

Raymond Foye Beta who executor & "We made a spiritual island in the name in honor of Rabelais & Crowley"

"ESOPUS" was a river in Greek mythology (its nymph was raped by Zeus) & a local Algonkin Indian tribe, so-called by the Dutch, who tried to exterminate them.

PLW

So much is fact, more or less. Legends however began to accrue, perhaps distortions of tall tales Crowley himself told the locals. One such legend mutated into a yarn in which AC canoes ashore one night and climbs Illinois Mt. (in the town of Lloyd, Ulster Co.) to a rock shelter known as Indian Cave; there he attempts to invoke a demon—whereupon suddenly Father Divine (the famous Black evangelist who settled in Ulster Co. with his followers in the 1930s) anachronistically appears and engages AC in a spiritual duel. Crowley is bested, and skulks off to Lake Minnewaska, where further adventures occur.

In 2005 I discovered that a local historian I know happens to be the grand-daughter of the farmer who owns Indian Cave on Illinois Mt., and so we paid it a visit. Not only did it make a perfect Gothick set-&-setting for the story— we also found the initials "A. C." among the graffiti carved on the roof of the shelter! In 2007 I organized an excursion (by rented sailboat) to Esopus Island, with Raymond Foye (of Hanuman Books) and William Breeze, the present head of Crowley's Ordo Templi Orientis and AC's official literary executor. In a fit of inspiration, acting as Frater Hymenaeus Beta, Bill claimed spiritual possession of the Island in the name of the *Thelemite Pantisocracy*, an ad-hoc combo of Crowleyan doctrine with the romantic scheme of Coleridge and Southey, *et al.*, to found a utopian commune in America in 1794. (Sadly the plan fizzled.) We hope someday to organize an *Order of Esopus Island*, based on these principles, open to all poets, artists, magicians and descendents of the Esopus Indians (the island's original owners, after all).

In 2009 I was invited by Hans Ulrich Obrist to contribute to a volume he's curating on "Maps for the 21st Century." For this project I made a psychotopographical map-collage of Esopus Island; subsequently I produced 3 more such maps.

Meanwhile, from 2004 onwards I've been involved with the cause of GREEN HERMETICISM. Our notion is that the alchemy of Paracelsus and his spiritual descendants the Romantic Scientists — Novalis, Goethe, Joseph Priestley (another Pantisocrat, by the way) or Sir Humphrey Davy — might offer a philosophic matrix for contemporary ecological science, one that links it to the Greco–Egypto-Pagano-Jewish-Christian-Islamic Renaissance Hermetic tradition, but also to experimental ("Modern") science as developed by such Rosicrucians, Freemasons and alchemists as Bacon, Newton, Descartes, Boyle, and most of the Royal Society.

Ideally, Green Hermeticism would realize "the poeticization of science," as Novalis put it. But as a non-scientist I began to consider other possible ways of moving Green Hermeticism beyond mere written theory and toward some kind of actual practice.

Thus I came up with the idea of poetic action, that is, non-verbal poetry, in the form of *Vanishing Art,* my term for art that only exists in the moment of its disappearance. Based on ten years of research into local magical lore and insurrectionary history of the Hudson Valley, I wanted also to combine *narration* with visual art, like the "art pompier" and History painters of the 19th century such as John Martin and Thomas Cole. So each action would be documented with a poem or hand-calligraphed essay, photographs, archival material, etc. (in a Box) and also with at least one chartomantic ideo-collage (or "cartolage") in the form of a Map like those I'd made for Esopus Island. (The Map is not the Territory — and yet it is.) The actions would not be carried out as "Performance" nor as "Hermetic Ritual," but would be influenced by these, as well as by Situationist Psychogeography; Conceptual Art; Beuysian "social sculpture"; Land Art; the Benjaminian/Surrealist "Profane Illumination"; as well as specific influences from Indo-Persian geomancy (especially the siting of tombs); plus a lot of slogging around Wisconsin studying Indian Effigy Mounds, and around Ireland studying Megaliths; frequently under the aegis of certain plants of power, the "devas" or Nature Elementals as entheogens. These plants have their own agenda, of course, which can be described as both radical and green.

The ecological alchemy attempted here (or at least hoped for) involves the *re-enchantment of a landscape* that is threatened now not just by the disenchantment of vulgar materialism but also by its consequences, including at best the poisoning of landscape or its reduction to mere image-of-itself as artefact of consumerist "Green" or "Heritage Tourism"; at worst — a parking-lot stretching into infinity.

Thus these actions typically partake of the nature of mourning (elegiac epitaph) but also of *pilgrimage*. The tourist merely vampirizes and nullifies the magic of place; the pilgrim however donates magic faith to the shrine and receives blessing in return. In America nature has always been our shrine for the most part; we were meant to be animists. We must consider the possibility of re-paganizing monotheism in order to conceive of living space as it once existed for, say, the Esopus Indians.

I envision what I call a *"santeria,"* a syncretistic religion in which Egypto-Greco-Roman deities are identified with Hindu devas, African orishas, and Christian saints, in a kind of hoodoo infused with *el Spirito Indio* (both Native American and Tantrik), and even Islamic (there exist certain trickster spirits called "Turks" in Brazilian Candomblé). I can venerate the Christian saints thanks to my Anglican baptism, and the spirits thanks to my several initiations, including the Moorish Orthodox Church, Bengali Tara Tantra, and various Sufi Orders. As for the manitous, the Native spirits — they come with the landscape. This "religion" will take shape inside the artworks & cantos of the poem; it is the metaphysical aspect of them.

Sopus, in the language of the Waranawarongkong natives of what is now Ulster Co., meant something like riverpeople, the river in question being the very same one the Dutch named Esopus, I think as a double-Dutch pun on the famous Esopus (or Asopus or Aesopus) River of ancient Greece. Combining the Greek mythology of that River with the local Indian mythology & history (what little can now be recovered), plus other folklore & history, gave me my cast of characters, gods & goddesses of Nature in revolt against Heaven itself, and re-incarnating over time as various human heroes — *viz:* Big Indian, Oscar Wilde, Dr Brink, Becky de Milt, and numerous numinous nymphs, undines and Elementals, spearcarriers & fictional or fragmentary extras, soon to appear.

After each event/place/Canto of the poem I include a "Press Release" written to describe the Vanishing Art Work carried out at that locus (the dates are not sequential — I had to do these things when possible, not as I'd perhaps ideally prefer). There I mention some of the many friends who've helped me reconnoiter, plan, move across real or imagined (or cyber) 'scapes of various sorts; friends who've witnessed the actions (a necessary part of the art), photographed them, written about them, allowed them to take place on their private land, or otherwise aided & abetted. The title *riverpeople* was suggested by Robert Kelly.

I didn't manage to do an artwork for the Ashokan Canto due to difficulty of access. The event envisioned for the Saugerties Lighthouse Canto proved prohibitively expensive! Anyone who'd like to fund it please contact me c/o the Publisher.

In Sept.–Oct. 2012 my art — both Esopus and non-Esopus — was exhibited in New York at the 1:1 Gallery (i.e., "one-to-one"), under the title "Vanishing Art & Hoodoo Metaphysics" (see www.1to1ny.com). In this connection I'd like to tip the fez to Jarrett Earnest & the 1:1 Gallery staff; Phong Bui of *The Brooklyn Rail* & his staff & students; Hans Ulrich Obrist, agnes b, and the staff of *point d'ironie;* Mick Taussig, Carolee Schneemann, Sterrett Smith & David Levi Strauss, Raymone Foye, and Kim Spurlock.

E. A. Poe complained that long poems inevitably have prosy bits & even boring sections — so I have tried to do those parts as honest prose. Slipping back-and-forth between poetry & prose is a form of practise I picked up gradually while co-translating Persian & Urdu texts, such as the *Divine Flashes* of Fakhroddin 'Iraqi, which mix prose & poetry into a "new" genre that, as far as I know, has no name in any language, not even Persian or Greek. Perhaps it might be called the *museon,* since (at least in the present case) nearly all nine Muses have participated in it.

Ralph Albert Blakelock, "Catskill Mountain Landscape"

Canto I/1
Invocation

Swing ah Muse the Temporary
                                       Neo-Pastoral Zone
Seven Stations of martyrdom
Seven Revelations
                  & as many Pic-nics
                  on greenswards w/ lutenists
                  jazz fruiterers etc.
bearing watermelons apples pears apricots
peaches grapes cherries persimmons
pomegranates broken open like Romanov
Easter eggs of Christ's Blood figs
                                            beach-plums
blood shed for us by 13 pagan Christs
incl. Apollo Dionysus & Nietzsche

Voudou blood
cacogenic blood
                  of impure Saints
                        & failed or even
                                false messiahs
Failure as the Last Possible Outside
                                        — that
2nd coming inexplicably delayed from circa
70 AD to now — the No-Show Guy
the dead guy.
You have to have the disease yourself
    in order to recognize it
                                    — bad blood
Jukes-&-Kallikaks messiahs
                          Swamp Angels
                              in bat caves

Have you seen Earth turn a little in sleep
tossing aside blankets of dead snow & leaves
icicle'd as some hibernating toad

                              yet alive & dreaming
have you seen a mountain stream
no matter how often martyred
w/ dams sewage outlets algic bloom
clean itself w/ energy vortices —
nordic runic spiral snake
shedding past forms re-making itself
                                        a-new
bluegreen ice-hexagonal attractors
sparkling epiphanic

Think like Goethe — dare to be wrong
yet justified in the eyes of
uncountable angelic beings.
If our pagan deities have withdrawn
                          grown silent
we should do no less
                  Retreat
                  to some monastery
            in Hardenburgh & pray
for mycroremediation
                  wherever relatively unscathed
                                    druid groves
have outlasted Progress & escaped the gaze
of the pyramidical panopticonic
                  Ponzi scheme called Civilization
e.g. the old-growth hemlock
                  at Otter Falls

drunk on water
old sufi paradox — so attuned
      by concatenation of Moon & Mercury
                        to H_2O
as living entity
            nymph-haunted
      self-healing
                        lizard's tail
undinic hydromancy springs forth
from Jove's brow spontaneously
an occult art or science generated
by the text itself
Muse-driven rhapsodic
                  episodic
                  epistemic
dowsing the Ulster Co. Atlas

to trace an aqua-chorography of pure blue lines
(like that human nervous system
transmuted to quicksilver, 18th cen.,
               in the Naples Museum)
a dragon pinned down by a
dozen St George lances but
               still flowing
outwardly pure Yin but inwardly
    Winter as the very principle
             of élan vital.
You can't kill the stuff.
             I remember
growing up beside another Leni Lenape
tribal river the Raritan in a
dead ruined 19th cen. industrial town
with abandoned canal & Lovecraftian
redbrick factories boarded up
in the Number One heavy-metal pollution corridor
of 1950s USA — a river reputedly
not just defunct but poisonous —
             & some biologist
from Rutgers discovered a kind of opposum
believed extinct for a million years
living on the towpath near my house

Mr Emoto even claims water has emotions
& shows photos where good thoughts
turn stagnant water into living
             psychedelic jewelry
I've witnessed filthy garbage soup turned into
pure drinking water by New Alchemy Institute
                    zero-energy
rock/plant/water flow systems. Note
Le Comte de Gabalis says Undines
    of all Elementals are most eager
             for love with humans
See also Baron de La Motte-Fouqué's
    Undine & opera by E.T.A. Hoffmann
witness human intercourse with Silkies
seal-maidens in Scotland & Japan
Melusine in South France — Hylas
             & the Water Nymphs
in the *Argonautica* — the eros of water
its spermatic universality its Neptunic
orgone-blue depths — blue champagne.

Including a Guide to Semi-Secret
Swimming Holes — not for publication.
Eyes Only — unknown to damn tourists
or other scopophiliac image-vampires. Publication
profanes secrets meant for manuscript
or oral transmission, without which
knowledge is merely data. Facts
handwritten or spoken have at least
the bare chance of enchantment —
    of becoming Poetic Facts. Or
        if you must use print
use it poorly
    in crackpot tracts or shoddy
    leaflets by local antiquarian cranks
    or slender vol's of poetry w/ tasteful covers
but best would be poems that
don't even use words — poems
that are acts — that vanish in
the very moment of their appearance —
evanescent as breezes but inshallah
resonant as bombs.
    Acts w/ repercussions.
Art meant primarily for invisible spirits
& therefore already GONE.
      Occult manipulations of
       chartomantic ideolages
    (because the Map is Not the Territory

                    — and yet
                      it is)

the Map is all Signatures — each
with its planetary or zodiacal sign
its Lunar Mansion or Fixed Star
every map has its night sky.

Esopus Creek
demands all 9 Muses, viz.:

                    Calliope — heroic epic
        with   Clio — history
        Apollo   Euterpe — flutes
        on Mt   Terpsichore — lyric & dance
        Helicon   Erato — hymns
        acc. to   Melpomene — tragedy
        Hesiod   Thalia — comedy
                    Polyhymnia — mimesis
                    Urania — astronomy

Plus: Seven Planetary Deities
    Seven African Powers
    Seven Eyes of Allah
    Seven Rishis or Wisemen
    Seven Stars in Ursa
    Seven Stars in Pleiades
    Lucky Seven
Plus
    Shiva Bhole
    Tara
    Khezr
    Lal Shabazz Qalandar
    St Anthony of Egypt
    Ma Ku
    Hermes (Budh)
    Soma
& a Cast of other dozens
to be unveiled Canto by Canto

under the special patronage of
    MAYSINGWEY
Lord of the Hunt & Cosmic Bear
in the Land of the Warranawonkong
       & the Wall of Manitou.

Thomas Cole, "The Clove, Catskills"

Canto I/2

Ideological Collage or
Super-Imposition of the
Mantic Chorography of the
Esopus Waters
on a Hydraulic Map of Ulster Co.:
Winnisook to Phoenicia

essentialism — to say for example
    Irish Catskills or Neanderthal Liberation Front
           or OD or VRIL or PHLOGISTON
                gives off such a thrill
of forbidden irridentist revanchist
        shoe fetishism
— the New Endarkenment —
    the insipid slothful zen
          of flyfishing while under
             the Influence

                Summer Camp of the Unnameable
                Bungalows of Indio Ghosts
                Kuchalein Kabins for Frankist Kabbalists
                Whispering Hemlock Weekly Rentals
                meandering along the wide veranda
                  eyes blanked out
                      with impermissable distillates
                        of distant stars

(haiku)
    Up in Frost Valley
        Sure enough we found some frost
           Just as we had hoped

            The Esopus's tragic fate
is foretold at its very birth — where the
natal spring has been dammed & supped into
an artificial lake under the Indio name
            Winnisook

with chainlink fence around gated
vacation community of annoying joggers —
it creeps under the road & bursts out
down the vast V of Hemlock Mt.
purging itself of bourgeois pollutants
tapping water table's tentacles
of stolen freshets to become
                              Otter Falls
virgin stand of cyclopean hemlocks
preserved by inaccessibility from
19th cen. satanic tanneries like
icon of Nature as God by Blakelock
or Innes — thick plush mattress
of moss pure DMT hallucinations
four waterfalls & a swimming hole
worthy of Niebelungen Jungwandervögel
negative ionization of air 100%
cut with biblical
        balsam — swords of sunlight
                                    slice
our joss-stick smoke — palpable
presence of Naiad or Rivergod as
            divine adolescent

Highest-Clarity Mao Shan School draws
a map of magic mountains each
hollowed out like those realms
accessible in Irish lore by diving into
enchanted forest pools — Eyes
            of the Otherworld —
            & takes that map like a
            net of jewels & casts it
            over the sleeping form
                of China or
                        Upstate NY
in a choromantic spell
                of akashic cartography
or geophrenology coordinating earth's sacred
                            bumps & orifices
w/ invisible landscape of the *Alam-i Mithal*
or *Mundus Imaginalis* vastly enhancing
already heart-breaking beauty of
everything transitory manifesting
                fragile tao

in a town
called Big Indian, with its
concrete teepee & kitsch Colossus out on
Route 28 since 1957, its
concrete stupa built by
           Swami Rudrananda
crumbles into yet another Instant Ruin
forlorn up Lost Clove Road abandoned
after the Seventies in a field of weeds
w/ bits of Buddhist temples looted in Laos
& Rudy's statue wrapped in enigmatic plastic
                    (it might be anyone)
                         larger than death

In Phoenicia however no concrete ziggurat
to Baal or Temple of Cybele is to be seen
not even a Melkart Street or Mammon Avenue
or winged bull demon with vitreous beard
or Lilith of the Euphrates
                    — too bad
because concrete used to be the
ectoplasm of America's pop surrealist *imaginaire*
buildings shaped like elephants or ducks
or hotdogs or Egyptian tombs
                    cement was alchemized
from psychic bunker authoritarianism
to free play concrete gardens in Wisconsin
Turkish kiosks in Wildwood NJ
Gaudi cement not Bauhaus concrete
of the machine-for-living — no — but Rosendale cement
as in the Brooklyn Bridge the first
adorable dream of Modernismo — so —
raise gimcrack gothick castles along holy Hudson
ferro-concrete pyramids in Cairo (Greene County)
cement miniature-golf-style repro's
           of Irish megaliths in East Durham
eccentric selftaught crackpot country visionaries
w/ concrete Beulah-lands & Cockaignes
in their front yards — *floreant omnes* —
           1000 flowers bloom.

Canto 1/3
Hardenburgh

Don't get me started on the Hardenburgh Patent
O Muse — "Nine generations of Kingston laswyers
have sharpened their fangs on the Hardenburgh Tract"
                              (—Alf Evers)
grand slam land scam & shame of Ulster Co.
Lord Cornbury (in drag) receives Johannes Hardenburgh
sells off 1½ million acres — most of the Catskills
in a fell swoop — Esopus Indians with flintlocks chase away surveyors
Hardenburgh and his cronies sell huge chunks to Robert Livingston
rat-capitalist bastard of Clermont Manor (the patroonship
against which Anti-Rent War will be fought
two centuries later). Feudal demesne. Forest primeval.

Squatters runaways hermits tax evaders
White Indians. Calico Indians.
Last of the Esopus Indians.
Haunted stone farmhouse. Face of a murdered slave
seen at upstairs window. (One of Hardenburgh's grandsons
owned Sojourner Truth.) Another Hardenburgh
a gouging mean landlord got shot in the back
riding home on a lonely road somewhere in the Tract
a crime never solved beneath the Moon.

One single-lane road goes into Hardenburgh &
                              doesn't come out
nothing to see there except no-postal-service zones
bewilderness — the trail leads to Tunis Lake
then over Hemlock Mt. to Frost Valley
source of our ESOPUS and RONDOUT creeks
100's of sq. miles all green — perfect for Tarzan or the Baron in the Trees
green as green can be
              the cougars are back
or whatever you call the original
                              Katskill cats

Forests are back. And why? Why?
       I'll tell you why.
Because the Rockefellers bought up every
            fucking acre
of Hardenburgh except for a few gores & corners
for a dozen or so friends & relatives
forced out the farmers with money
          "prices that couldn't
            be refused"
said the last shopkeeper in Hardenburgh bitter woman
alone in tiny rural grocery w/ no visible neighbors
"everyone sold and left."
    "And you, ma'am?"
        "I refused" — w/ a grim smile.

And two monasteries out Beaver Kill Rd.
one Buddhist one Xtian — no fair dammit —
          enlightenment
must be automatic there — breathe it
in with the air — rich ozone of
          undeveloped property
an Eden fenced with money & power
          forever green.
          Beat Zen
          neo-survivalists
backpack into Hardenburgh & stay the whole summer
squatting on public trails & wandering
off to waterfalls & caves poaching a few deer
muskrat squirrel mushrooms ginseng
to sell for a bit of cash to buy bacon
          coffee
wine sugar tinned milk — grow a patch of
          hemp somewhere
play Robin Hood to the Rockefeller's
          Sheriff of Nottingham
expropriating the expropriators' *satori* practising
Animal Kung Fu in limpid dawn meadows

such as the one where I picnic'd with poet Sparrow
& Professor Boon of Psychedlic Studies Dept. & his
fiancée now wife Christy w/ baby Rabindranath
toasted NOVALIS whose real name of course
was von *Hardenberg* — easy to summon up
in this schwartzwald between Delaware
          & Hudson watersheds

where the 18th century seems as plausible
as any other.

        Wolf Turtle Turkey & Crow
are the moieties or sub-clans of the Esopus
             (later "Munsee") Indians
"but the Crows were greatly reduced
in number & consigned to minor role of
lighting ceremonial pipes for Wolves" — *les loups*
as the Canadians called them.
Adopted as Crow & Keeper of the Pipe
we might go *low* as alchemical Nigredo
corn-thief & roadkill gourmet — in trance
to fly & laugh —
        sounds OK.

A harebrained winter excursion to Hardenburgh
in the middle of a snowstorm.
        Sunset like an iron curtain
              burnished with snow
seeing it from the window
        of yr monkish cell
          monkish fungi
            cinnabar elixirs.
Camp Graf von Hardenberg in the spook infested
Catskills — the Novalis Institute
          hidden behind thick
            forest
wall of snow-bent zen pines & whispering hemlocks
w/ their air of immortality but not
        caring

after midnight the snow clears
leaving milky way aurora borealis
virtually unstained by any pink glow
        of Civilization.
Sanctity oozes out of the weather itself
primitive involvement with burning wood
swirling incense steaming tea
those morphological paradigms
of perfect nature as Perfect Nature —
a natural & even creative error
        a necessary error
a fortuitous misunderstanding
        that resolves itself

on a higher gyre: a temporary monkery
— and —
    the romance of real estate as
      esoteric sub-text of all
          American psycho-history
1776 Revolution basically a real estate scam
gone sour. Stars & stripes are the
Washington family coat of arms. Wake up America.
King George & His Vizier Alexander Hamilton.
Millions of acres of Indian-infested
              virgin Atlantis.
Illuminati get-rich-quick schemes.
        Our religion of Nature
endlessly exorcizes from its entrails the
        illusion of feudal dues
the Spectral alienation of Property
      versus the mutualism
        of usufruct.

The only cure for envy & ressentiment
is proprietorship. I must myself
      own Hardenburgh.

Calico Indian Jungwandervögel armed shamans
& shamanettes of anti-Capitalismo
Stirnerite Greenshirts from the Cercle Proudhon
Green Mountain types w/ dogs & rifles
the Hardenburgh Peoples Militia
           Novalis Brigade
Nietzsche Brigade — Oscar Wilde Brigade —
          nudist foodcranks
tree huggers with guns. I invoke
these figures yet fear them —
      green puritans
      fanatics.
I am dynamite said Nietzsche wistfully.
Up in the Zoroastrian Alps
w/ Whitmanesque prerequisite comrades
         of the heart
free love — lute music — roast venison
trespassers in paradise.
      A Revery
while snowed in here by whale-oil lamplight
laudanum 10¢ a bottle
      snow & opium

dream of 1907 or 1911 or thereabouts
this nest of Jukes — poachers &
                    moonshiners
guaranteed endarkenment.

Thomas Bewick, "Man on Stilts Walking Through a Stream, Followed by a Dog"

Canto 1/4
Big Indian

Winneesook was a seven-foot-tall Munsee living in the Esopus Valley near Marbletown. Winneesook means "snowfall," but the white people called him "big Indian." He fell in love with Miss Gertrude Molyneux, a proper lady of the town. At first she was embarrassed by his dramatic overtures, for he lived in the woods, but after a while it was clear that she was getting very interested. Her parents became hostile and forced her to marry a Mister Joseph Bundy, a man of means capable of protecting her from the "savage." But Gertrude had a mind of her own, and did not find Joseph to her liking. She eloped one night with the "big Indian," and they escaped into the woods together and settled down to raise a family in the wilderness. Gertrude's parents continued to complain of the captive state of their daughter, but to no avail.

Several years passed, and when someone's cow disappeared, certain people spead rumors that it was "that big Indian!" Joseph Bundy, still seeking revenge for the loss of his wife, led the charge. They found Winneesook and chased him for miles until they reached what is now Big Indian, New York. According to the story, Joseph called out, panting, "I think… the best way to civilize… that yellow serpent… is to let daylight into his heart!"

Joseph raised his rifle and fired. Big Indian staggered to the hollow of an old pine tree where he hid for a while. Gertrude found him there and held him upright in her arms until he died, as her ex-husband looked on without remorse. Gertrude and her children moved to that spot to tend his grave, and they formed the nucleus for the future town of Big Indian. It is handed down that the tree remained standing as a local landmark and was often pointed out to visitors to Big Indian until the 1880s, when it was cut down to make a railroad embankment. — Evan T. Pritchard, *Native New Yorkers: The Legacy of the Algonquin People of New York* (2002).

Just as the entire Esopus River seems falsifed by the rape of its source & transformation into the gated vacation community of Lake Winnisook so too the figure of Winneesook himself — Big Indian — (the name means "Snow-Falling-Reflected-in-His-Eyes," according to my source*) has been twisted every which way. That he was seven or 7½ feet tall seems likely given the number of "giant" skeletons found all over Turtle Island & the mysterious ritual importance of their graves. I studied a burial at Atzlan in Wisconsin where an "Indian princess" clad entirely in seashells was found entombed flanked by two 7-foot giants, one hunchback boy & a turtle. The grave had been cov-

---

*In Lenape myth Snow Boy sacrifices himself, but "returns" in winter so his people may easily track game.

ered by a 2-ton boulder as if to prevent escape which according to my HoChunk ("Winnebago") informants was literally true, since the "Princess" had invaded the northwoods "Driftless" region from Mississippean "Southern Death Cult" & practised witchcraft & cannibalism — her ghost had to be pinned down.

Anyway — giants in the Earth in them days — but the story of Big Indian and "Gertrude" begins to look shaky when we discover that "her" Indian name was *Aweesewa* since Aweesewa is clearly a boy's name & in fact was a wellknown Munsee leader whose elder brothers had gone to England on a famous embassy voyage to see Queen Anne. (According to Pritchard, Aweesewa was short & delicate & his eyes were "like pools of ink.") It appears that later in life Aweesewa lived with comrade-lover Winneesook acc. to my Indian informant who shall go unnamed — all the Eastern Woodlands peoples, he says, shared sacred traditions of same-sex partnerships documented later and more thoroughly farther West. The Dutch would doubtless've seen them as savage satanic sodomites, which might explain why they had to flee Marbletown for the wilds of Hardenbergh Mts., and shed light on the murder of Big Indian.

It's incorrect to speak only of berdache* transvestites or "squaw men" altho they play vital role of cosmic mediation & always represent shamanic or mediumistic powers. There also existed männerbunden with warrior shapeshifter ethos that excluded women (like the Corinthian Legion or the Spartans), as well as an "Orphic" tradition of mentor & ephebe like those rooted in primordial Dorian/Indo-European cults eventually culminating in Platonism & Persian Sufism.

"The unnatural is also the natural" as Goethe put it. Monotheisitic heterosexist authoritarian moralic acid in all its dreary pseudo-scientific secularized guises such as psychiatry begins to look like an actual disease — twisted & unnatural compared to the wi(l)der perspectives of paganism where every possible form of true love is considered sacred, presided over by guardian spirits, & good for the crops.**

Queer means uncanny — living in the liminal — un(ac)countable.

Queer isn't even about sex. Think of expressions like "woods-queer" or: "I say, Petrie old chap — there's something a bit queer here in this mummy-case... ARRGH!" or "queered his pitch" or The Pastoral is queer not so much because Theocritus & Virgil like boys but because pastoral vision comprises the "unnatural" yearning gaze that an alienated urbanized soul casts at a partially-imagined but also authentic Arcadian *eros*, a love-relation with *Nature's whole person* experienced as lost but recoverable thru poetry itself

or — was Thoreau queer?

or — how queer was Thoreau?

---

* Probably the only Persian word to enter North American Indian terminology. It means a boy beloved, but became French 18th cen. slang for catamite.

** The berdache is "sterile" — but the presence of the berdache "brings luck." See Will Roscoe, *Changing Over: Third & Fourth Genders in Native North America,* which also treats traditional lesbian relations.

Legal but boring, married, 9-to-5, gadgets galore, join the army — queers lost their magic along with the rhetoric of liberation. Homosexuals today need some André Breton or Guy Debord to expell them from the party for bourgeois deviation, betrayal of Dionysian principles. What's yr angle of stance vis-á-vis the universe — have you been fey today— have you seen the world vatically as an inspired bard — have you been uncanny — are you queer for Gaia — for the Green Carnation?

Isn't the unnatural also...the supernatural?

Have you emulated the devas, drunk the Soma, written the amulet, been the poem itself? Have you considered that without outsiders there is no Outside, no blank spot on the map, no Escape from the mechan/ASM & its Totality of managed consciousness...

Was Blake queer?

The site of the pine tree beneath which Winneesook expired which was cut down in the 1880s for a railway embankment should be detectable thru combination of cod archeology & stoned dowsing... I can see it now; very taoist... twisted & suggestive of other dimensions — a rack to hang scarves of mist on — a sentient being, that pine. And now it's absent — like the Indians themselves — but not quite dead — gone elsewhere — to Hell or Oklahoma — and that invisible stump would make an appropriate esoteric pilgrimage site for Vanishing Art homage to Big Indian, saint & martyr... of unmentionable love...

How to put this politely...

The Esopus Indians...

were a superior race

— not by eugenics or genetics or blood but by way of life. Their defeat was a sign of their Election. Roughly speaking humans were clearly meant to live more-or-less like Esopus Indians, i.e., neolitihic hunting/gathering/gardening — no metal — population steady — nature bountiful — no writing — no State — no Xtian morals — rivers swimming with eels & trout, air dazzled with gamebird wings, forest seething w/ major mammals, earth — the Three Sisters (corn beans squash) — mountains for vision quests — the Sublime, as Burke put it.

Winter for narrative, summer for adventure, moving steadily as breezes over the earth, leaving no trace —

clearly this is roughly the normal life for the present cusp of evolution's wave — not Civilization. Humans were meant for paradise not Moloch & Mammon

— so today

— I'd say

we come here to pray at the unseen grave of Winneesook, not only in mourning but to learn.

Press Release
Vanishing Art #4
Sun. May 30, '10 Saint Maguil's Day
"Big Indian"

According to legend Winnisook or "Big Indian" was a giant 7½-foot-tall Esopus Indian from around Hurley who (sometime in the 18th century) was forced to flee up into the Catskills after he married a white woman. Her ex-husband finally tracked him down and murdered him and he was buried in what is now the hamlet of Big Indian, founded by his grieving widow.

According to a more historical account — which agrees with Indian oral tradition as well — Winnisook's lover was actually a man, Aweesewa, a respected diplomat, older (and shorter) than Winnisook, possibly a sort of *berdache* or crossdress shaman. If Big Indian was martyred by the Christians it may have been for the sin of sodomy rather than miscegenation. Either way, he appears as a Hero of Love.

"Lake Winnisook" today is an artificial lake created by damming the spring that is the source of the Esopus River — the first of many wounds inflicted on this beautiful body of water, starting with the defeat and banishment of the Sopus Indians who lived along its meanders, later the Ashokan Dam & Reservoir, the Kingston dike, Hurricane Irene, etc.

Last winter I drafted a huge seven-canto-long mixed poetry-&-prose text all about the Esopus River, its hydrography, topology and history. Canto I concerns Big Indian as the source of the river. Each Canto is planned to become the "documentation" for a Vanishing Artwork, which I will carry out (not necessarily in sequence) over the next year or two, inshallah; viz:

II. Oscar Wilde in the Catskills

III. The Ashokan Dam Allegorized as the Rape of Aegina Daughter of Esopus by Zeus in the Form of the U.S. Eagle

IV. Swimming Holes

V. Dr. Brink vs. The Woodstock Witches

VI. The Esopus Wars

VII. The Lighthouse at Saugerties

The tentative title for the whole work is *riverpeople* — a literal transation of Algonkian *'sopus* with a double-dutch pun on the Classical Greek myth of the River Esopus.

Ideally I would have liked to carry out the first act at the source of the River, but "Lake Winnisook" makes that impossible. Instead I chose Otter Falls, just downsteam from the source, a site not shown on any map and unmarked by any sign: a grove of climax-growth hemlock (the original Catskill forest) with banks of moss 3-ft. deep, four waterfalls and a swimming hole, all in perfect "Hudson River School" taste, unspoiled and obviously still sacred.

That Sunday fell in the middle of Memorial Day weekend — the whole region was swarming with tourists — weather ideal, about 78° with blue sky and swift white clouds — and yet we were utterly alone at Otter Falls for about two hours — not one hiker interrupted us.

My "temporary landscape installation" took place under the exoteric sign of the Sun but the esoteric signs of Moon & Mercury. This combination evoked the African-American *orisha* of freshwater streams and medicinal herbs, called *Inle* in Santeria (in Cuba & NYC) and *Simbi* in Haitian/N. Orleans Voudoun. He is syncretized with the Archangel Raphael (a lunar/hermetic-type Healer) and the youth Tobit (in the Apocrypha). Inle–Raphael is considered the patron *Santo* of same-sex love. I interpret Winnisook — Big Indian himself — as an avatar of Inle and thus a Saint in the secret Afro-Algonkan-Anglican *Santeria* or hoodoo that forms my occult matrix for *re-paganization of monotheism and re-enchantment of landscape*.

So — after offering tobacco for Native Spirits and rose agarbhatti for the Sun — in my capacity as Metropolitan (Moorish Orthodox Church of America), Doctor of Divinity & Druid (Universal Life Church of Modesto, Calif.), etc., I burned five incenses: special blends for Mercury & Moon, then Myrtle, Mandrake and Myrrh; the "5M's" are meant to evoke the Five Sacraments of Left-Hand Tantra, including ritual intercourse, i.e. sex magic. Then I made sacrifice to the nymphs, undines & rivergods of the Esopus in Celtic style (by sacrifice in water) of the following items:

1) Five Silver Coins: a 1-oz. Chinese "Panda" with Temple of Heaven; a ½-oz. Chinese "Mouse" with 8 Trigrams & Yin-Yang disc; a 1-oz. Chinese calligraphic piece; a 1-oz. Mexican "10 Pesos" with Aztec Eagle & Snake; a ½-oz. Mexican "Peso" with Eagle/Snake and Liberty Cap with light-rays, looking *very* much like a magic mushroom. (All worth about $100 as bullion.)

2) Two large genuine baroque pearls and ten seed-pearls, from 47th street in Manhattan, worth about $75.

3) A "booklet" of pure silver foil or leaf, crumbled into bits.

4) A jar of white honey

5) A vial of ambergris

After the action and reading of the above statement (and a bit of R&R) we went looking for Big Indian's grave. At the town's general store the genial manager gave us vague directions — "Go up Lost Hollow to a fork in the road." According to Pritchard's *Native New Yorkers* the crooked pine-tree under (or in?) which Winnisook was buried was cut down when the railroad reached the hamlet in the 19th century. We located the old tracks in the village. We then drove up Lost Hollow. At the fork (actually a crossroads) we got out of our cars. Chuck suggested we all (six of us) put our fingers on his "magic walkingstick" and see if it pointed anywhere. While we were thus engaged an old lady emerged from her house to see what the heck we were up to. *By chance she happened to be* the retired Town Historian, who at once pointed us in the right direction, "down Lasher Road at the ruined railway trestle" — the authentic folk-lore grave site. My psychic antennae (for what they're worth) told me Big Indian's remains were lying very near or even under the road directly between the Trestle's abutments.

We then paid a visit to the strange statue (kitsch? raw art?) of Winnisook in Big Indian's Town Park. A "stream" of iridescent glass pebbles in cement flows between his feet; one was loose and I stole it.

Thanks & Tips-o-the-fez to Raymond, Shiv, Rachel, Chuck, Nathan et al.
In Memoriam Peter Orlovsky (died that morning)
Save the Mountain

OTTER FALLS ART ACTION 5/29/10

Peter Lamborn Wilson is writing a magnum opus
    on the folklore & origins of the Esopus
research involves investigating the exact source
    of the river at Lake Winnisook in Big Indian
The art action was an elaborate offering to the actual Big Indian
Winnisook
Seven and a half feet tall
Who was allegedly brutally murdered by Colonialists
    and buried in a tall pine tree
for the crime of either marrying a white woman
    or for, more likely says Peter, living openly with his male lover

in this desolate hidden green forest
one can imagine the otters sliding down
    the wet mossy sloping waterfalls
    descending down into seven swirling whirlpools
    into the freezing black swimming hole
in this shady grove there were no otters
    but philosophers, professors, artists, anthropologists,
    tarot experts, poets, students & saints
    all gathering together artistically spiritually naturally

PLW, on that day, transformed into
    an ancient white bearded druid pagan Celtic-Moorish priest
Lit rose incense for the sun
Lit 5 incenses that start with the letter M
    symbolizing secret tantrik sex magick
offered 5 big solid silver coins to the foaming pools
& sheets of silver foil which floated on the breeze
    like the faded memories of the foggy past
& he offered a handful of translucent pearls
& a jar of pure white honey
& a vial of whale's ambergris oil
Essential oils for essential Catskill folklore
Essential nature knowledge for Indians, otters & everyone

SHIV MIRABITO

Oscar Wilde   Saint & Martyr

Canto II/1
Oscar Wilde in the Catskills

Part 1: Introduction: Queer Constellations, or
                    Famous Fags of Outer Space

(FOR SHIV MIRABITO)

"thought to have been named *Aquarius*
stands holding a wine-jar pouring
                    a stream of liquid:
Ganymede (and they call Homer to witness)
adjudged worthy by the gods was
                    carried away
on account of his beauty to be cup-bearer to Zeus
& was granted immortality (till then
                              unknown to men)
his drink resembles nectar of the gods
                    in 31 stars"
                    — Pseudo-Eratosthenes
                    Catasterismi, 26

"Aquila the eagle that snatched up Ganymede
to heaven to his lover Jupiter"

                    — Hyginus
                    Poeticon Astronomicon, 2.16

"During the reign of Hadrian an attempt was made to form a new constellation out
of six or seven stars in lower Aquila,
    to be called Antinous after the Bithynian youth
                              drowned in the Nile
Ptolemy records it & it persisted into
                    modern times"
                    — Theony Condos
                    Star Myths of the Greeks & Romans

Canto II/2
Oscar on the Esopus

Oscar Fingal O'Flaherty Wills Wilde
                                    Saint & Martyr
first graced our Catskill biosphere in 1882 up the
Hudson by luxury steamboat *Mary Powell*
then by Catskill Mt. Railway from
Catskill Landing to Kaaterskill Hotel
Aug. 15 to lecture on Decorative Arts
& gaze at the famous Falls — iconic emblem
of Romantic Hudson River School painters —
the *Sublime* — (& much nicer than
Niagara Falls which Oscar found dull & noisy)
with his friend & agent D'Oyly Carte
that evening someone in the crowd
pelted Oscar w/ a giant sunflower
                            dropped from a stairwell
whereupon he criticized the Hotel's china
but declared himself CHARMED by the Catskills
vowing to return.
                        Three days later the 18th
he graced the banks of holy Esopus
at Tremper House Hotel in Phoenicia
(probably via Ulster & Delaware RR from Kingston)
Oscar packed several Aesthetic Outfits with him
might've worn his green velvet knee britches
silk hose & silver-buckled patent leather
                                    black pumps
satin "smoking" or black evening tails w/
                                    white cravat
velvet Mexican cape & cowboy hat
                (gift of the miners in
                        Leadville, Colo.
                whom Oscar called the
                best-dressed men in America)
ivory cane kid gloves silver cigarette case
hair long proto-hippy style — maybe a lily

or sunflower in hand to annoy the
gawking bumpkins warned by newspapers
no redblooded American male
had any business approving of Wilde.

A rumor spread that he would speak
at Overlook Mt. House in Woodstock
a crowd gathered on the porch —
                    a stagecoach pulled up
— a cheer arose — and out stepped
local prankster "Boots" van Steenbergh
carrying an "Aesthetic" yellow umbrella
— the crowd disgusted melted away.
Meanwhile at Tremper House the real Oscar
might've been saying something like this:

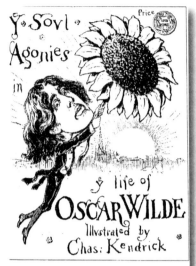

Decorative Art in America: A Lecture

"I do not want to shelter the movement which I have called 'The English Renaissance' under any palladium, however noble, or any name, however revered. The roots of it have indeed to be sought for in things that have long passed away, and not, as some suppose, in the fancy of a few young men — although I am not altogether sure that there is anything much better than the fancy of a few young men....

I speak for those whose desire for beautiful things is larger than their means. I find that one great trouble all over is that your workmen are not given to noble designs. You cannot be indifferent to this, because art is not something which you can take or leave. It is a necessity of human life....

I did not imagine until I went into some of your simpler cities that there was so much bad work done. I found where I went bad wall-papers, horribly designed, and coloured carpets, and that old offender, the horse-hair sofa, whose stolid look of indifference is always so depressing. I found meaningless chandeliers and machine-made furniture, generally of rosewood, which creaked dismally under the weight of the ubiquitous interviewer. I came across the small iron stove which they always persist in decorating with machine-made ornaments, and which is as great a bore as a wet day or any other particularly dreadful institution. When unusual extravagance was indulged in it was garnished with two funeral urns....

Perhaps one of the most difficult things for us to do is to choose a notable and joyous dress for men. There would be more joy in life if we should accustom ourselves to use all the beautiful colours we can in fashioning our own clothes. The dress of the future, I think, will use drapery to a great extent and will abound with joyous colour. At present we have lost all nobility of dress, and in doing so, have almost annihilated the modern sculptor. And in looking around at the figures which adorn our parks, one could almost wish that we had completely killed the noble art. To see the frock coat of the drawing-room done in bronze or the double waist-coat perpetuated in marble, adds a new horror to death....

In all my journeys through the country, the only well-dressed men that I saw — and in saying this I earnestly deprecate the polished indignation of your Fifth Avenue dandies — were the Western miners. Their wide-brimmed hats, which shaded their eyes from the sun and protected them from the rain, and the cloak, which is by far the most beautiful piece of drapery ever invented, may well be dwelt on with admiration. Their high boots, too, were sensible and practical. They wore only what was comfortable and therefore beautiful. As I looked at them, I could not help thinking with regret of the time when these picturesque miners should have made their fortunes and would go East to assume again all the abominations of modern fashionable attire. Indeed, so concerned was I that I made some of them promise that when they again appeared in the more crowded scenes of Eastern civilization they would still continue to wear their lovely costume. But I don't believe they will....

I do not see the wisdom of decorating dinner-plates with sunsets and soup-plates with moonlight scenes. I do not think it adds anything to the pleasure of the canvas-back duck to take it out of such glories. Besides, we do not want a soup-plate whose bottom seems to vanish in the distance. One feels neither safe not comfortable under such conditions....

The artist who goes to the children's playground, watches them at their sport, and sees the boy stoop to tie his shoe, will find the same themes that engaged the attention of the ancient Greeks, and such observation and the illustrations which follow will do much to correct that foolish impression that mental and physical beauty are always divorced.

To you more than perhaps to any other country, has nature been generous in furnishing material for art-workers to work in. You have marble-quarries where the stone is more beautiful in colour than the Greeks ever had for their beautiful work, and yet every day I am confronted with the great building of some stupid man who has used the beautiful material as if it were not precious almost beyond speech. Marble should not be used save by noble workmen. There is nothing which gave me a greater sense of barrenness in traveling through the country than the entire absence of wood-carving on your houses. Wood-carving is the simplest of the decorative arts. In Switzerland the little barefooted boy beautifies the porch of his father's house with examples of skill in this direction. Why should not American boys do a great deal more and better than Swiss boys?

There is nothing to my mind more coarse in conception and more vulgar in execution than modern jewelry. This is something which can be easily corrected. Something better should be made out of the beautiful gold which is stored up in your mountain hollows and strewn along your river beds. When I was at Leadville and reflected that all the shining silver I saw coming from the mines would be made into ugly dollars, it made me sad. It should be made into something more permanent.

When I was in San Francisco I used to visit the Chinese Quarter frequently. There I used to watch a great hulking Chinese workman at his task of digging, and used to see him every day drink his tea from a little cup as delicate in texture as the petal of a flower, whereas in all the grand hotels of the land, where thousands of dollars have been lavished on great gilt mirrors and gaudy columns, I have been given my coffee or my chocolate in cups an inch and a quarter thick. I think I deserved something nicer.

The art systems of the past have been devised by philosophers who looked upon human beings as obstructions. They have tried to educate boys' minds before they had any. How much better it would be in these early years to teach children to use their hands in the rational service of mankind! I would have a workshop attached to every school, and one hour a day given up to the teaching of simple decorative arts. It would be a golden hour for the children. And you would soon raise up a race of handicrafts-men who would transform the face of your country. I have seen only one such school in the United States, and this was in Philadelphia, and was founded by my friend Mr. Leland. I stopped there yesterday and brought some of the work here this afternoon to show you. Here are two discs of beaten brass: the designs on them are beautiful, the workmanship is simple and the entire result is satisfactory. The work was done by a little boy twelve years old. This is a wooden bowl, decorated by a little girl of thirteen. The design is lovely, and the colouring delicate and pretty. Here you see a piece of beautiful wood-carving, accomplished by a little boy of nine. In such work as this children learn sincerity in art. They learn to abhor the liar in art — the man who paints wood to look like iron, or iron to look like stone. It is a practical school of morals. No better way is there to learn to love Nature than to understand Art. It dignifies every flower of the field. And the boy who sees the thing of beauty which a bird on the wing becomes when transferred to wood or canvas, will probably not throw the customary stone. What we want is something spiritual added to life. Nothing is so ignoble that art cannot sanctify it."

(Note: The "Mr. Leland" mentioned & praised as an educator by Oscar was Charles G. Leland, sadly neglected genius Philadelphia author of works on Gypsy language, Etruscan witchcraft, Micmac Indian legends & their Norse parallels, occultism, etc. Someone should do a biog.)

Did Oscar wear his famous fur coat even
in August? — Catskill summer nights can be nippy
— he kept the coat all his life & later
asked for it to be sent to him in gaol
                                        — much later.
Did Oscar bathe in the Esopus? — not likely
as he hated all forms of physical exertion
wldve been horrified by modern fools in rubber
                                        inner tubes
smashing themselves senseless on Esopus rapids
but — did he *admire* the creek — of course.
                                CHARMING.
Did Oscar sanctify the Esopus w/ that word
did he consecrate the wild waters he found
                                so Aesthetic
with his holy glance —
                        so we believe.
Speaking ex cathedra now as
        Metropolitan, Moorish Orthodox Church
                Sacristan & Verger, Shrine of St Anthony of Egypt
                                (Non-Juring Anglican)
        Head Druid of Mombaccus Grove, Ancient Order of Druids
                        (Universal Life Church of Modesto, Calif.)
        etc.
We shall hold ceremonies to sanctify & canonize
Oscar Wilde Saint & Martyr on the banks
of Esopus — ritual & also Vanishing Artwork
temporary landscape installation ideally on Aug. 18
followed perhaps by banquet in some hopefully decent
                                        restaurant
near site of long-vanished Mt Tremper Hotel & reading
of this CANTO of *riverpeople*

                        dedicated to
memory of Catskill historian Alf Evers
                              & Ed Sanders of Woodstock
& also Merlin Holland grandson of Oscar Wilde
whom I met long ago in Tehran & visited in London
long before he began to publish old family papers
some of which I've used in this text
& Raymond Foye & Shiv Mirabito, Woodstock M.O.C. members
who happily happened to recall Wilde's Catskill visit
during our pilgrimage to Big Indian (see Canto I)
w/out which there'd be no Canto II.

                  "A gentleman never looks out the window"
                              — Oscar Wilde
Winter 1882–3 Wilde misspent in Paris
hanging around the Decadents who
                        hung around Verlaine
& Sarah Bernhardt — changing his style
from Aesthetic Apostle to disciple of
                  JK Huysmans & Gustave Moreau
changing his hairstyle to Neronian languid bangs
boyish straw boater & white waistcoat
with teenage Robert Sherrard
                              his future biographer
drinking absinthe & most likely
indulging in haschisch & opium
putting last touches on his first play
Vera, or the Nihilists — first sign
of Oscar's growing interest in Socialism & anarchism —
which was due to open in NYC the following summer.

Oscar arrived in Manhattan Aug. 3 1883
to make long story short *Vera* flopped
closed after 7 nights & 7 days of bad reviews —
total disaster.
                  Disconsolate Oscar fled
back to charming Catskills — as he'd promised —
he returned. Soon he found
                        consolation.

PEPPER
In researching OW in the Catskills I may be the first historian to notice a little affair of the heart suffered by Oscar during his second visit to the region — more or less
the whole month of September 1883.
   Was he just sulking over *Vera*? Far from it. So far as I can tell none of his biogra-

phers have ever bothered to investigate — no letters or interviews survive from that period — & it was only while browsing thru old archives of crumbling *Greene Co. Examiner Record* (Catskill NY Apr. 18 1953) that I found an article referenced in Van Zandt's history of the Catskill Mountain House: "In the 80s They All Came To The Mountain House" by Mabel Parker Smith (little old local history lady, or so I picture her) based on an interview w/ then-quite-elderly former Hotel guest, a Mrs Gill.

Why did Oscar hole himself up in this grandiose old hotel, first & original of all Catskill hotels, for an entire month, contenting himself with helping to produce a frivolous amateur musical complete with chorus of sunflowers? Mrs Smith & Mrs Gill & Mr Van Zandt never wondered. To me it appears quite obvious: he had a crush on young Pepper. Perhaps they'd first met at the Tremper House in Phoenicia — on the veranda overlooking the Esopus; but Pepper's mother & sister were bored at the Tremper House — it was losing the battle of fashionability — too near the noisy railroad my dear — we've decided to *ascend* to the Catskill Mountain House of famous Mr Beach — grandest & most picturesquely situated of all the Grand Hotels — resort of celebrities like Pres. Grant — purest air cleanest water — blahblahblah. Oscar thinks: I'll follow young Pepper — he ingratiates himself with the family — altogether now they shift up, up to the desirable clime.

> And on the broad piazza
> You could ev'ry evening spy
> Groups of gay young people
> Safe from Mother's eye

and surely one such "group" evading familial surveillance consisted of Oscar & Pepper — talking about poetry of course — one perfect summer — remembered it all his life. Would Pepper have worn a sailor suit like *Death in Venice*? Picture a daguerrotype in sepia tones…. Would he have been too old for a velvet Faunteleroy suit? I think not. Especially after meeting Oscar. Did Oscar tell Pepper Greek myths of Aesopus & Aegina — Zeus — the rape etc. — in pastoral Upstate zones so "charming" and pantheistic? Mother must've been incredibly naive as it seems everyone was in those halcyon days. Did Oscar tell Pepper about Greek Love? On those stretched-out September afternoons so nearly endlessly fading into mauve studded w/ fireflies — did Oscar give Pepper Champagne when Mother wasn't paying attention? oblivious as some Victoria Empress of the Unconscious?

Day after day Oscar postpones departure…. Why else is he lingering on in the Catskills if not for this wistful romance probably unconsummated & "platonic" as we used to say in high school in the 1950s.

Live orchestral music "After The Ball Was Over" spills out of the huge ornate stifling ballroom onto the crepuscular cool lawn. The most Romantic landscapes are the ones where love has proved intoxicating yet impossible — Venice — or Proustian hotels of Normandy closed for the season — or the melancholy of September in the Catskills. Did someone chance to see them kissing & betray them? In any case a kiss is already a kind of betrayal. Was it a farewell kiss?

Pepper looks "Grecian," athletic, fair and lithe. He's ebullient — peppery — enthusiastic — moves on the balls of his feet & tends to hop or skip when excited — about poetry for example — or a sunflower. The AH Sunflower of Blake or Whitman (whom Oscar kissed in New Jersey) or Ginsberg on the harmonium — the ultimate Paracelsian Signature — "weary of time." Another queer flower, like the narcissus, or lily, or orchid w/ its indelicate eytmology. Something's inherently queer about pastoral poetry — Theocritus — Virgil — or else quite *mad* like poor John Clare — carried away by the Queen of the Fairies for seven years. By the Erl-King.

Wilde, and probably his son, by James Edward Kelly, 1882.

All this was revealed to me by psychic archaeology — telemetric surveys of ley lines & forgotten desires — that live on in certain places like psychic remnants — the cliff where once the Mountain House stood, you can see all the way to Massachusetts, now gone, burned down (for the insurance, they say) in the 1970s — akashic fragments of ancient unrealized summer loves, lost tintypes of an ephebe in black w/ peaked cap & sunflower on the moonlit promenade burnt down to its cellars & now overgrown full of bramble roses — poison ivy — nettles — wildflowers — fungus & moss. These flowers ought to be included offered on yr altar Oscar, here in the Hudson River School of landscape as epiphany. Saint & Martyr. Sacred to the memory (now passed on in automatic trance) of late summer 1883 unreeled before the brain like magic lantern slides — like spirit photographs — gauzy & out-of-focus as memory itself. And any "facts" that might come along later & seem to dispute my flickering vision/version will be denounced as dirty lies — & in any case irrelevant. Bah. Esopus & his daughter Aegina have spoken thru my pen. It must be true.

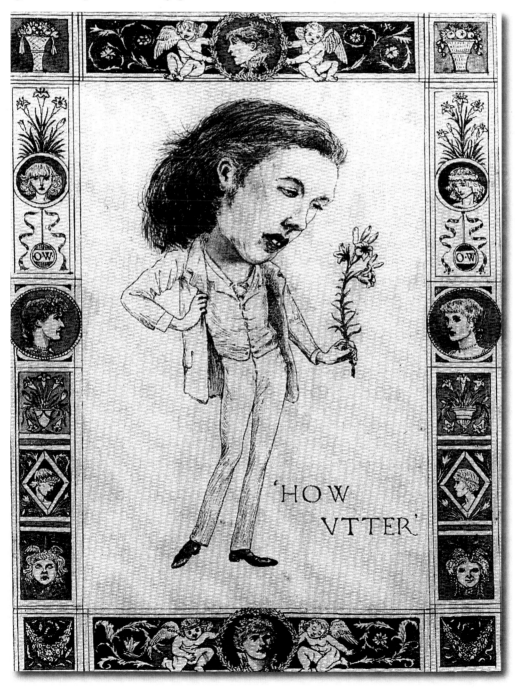

'HOW VTTER'

Canto II/3
Who Was George Wharton Pepper?

My neighbor Robert Kelly the poet remembers George Wharton Pepper as the crusty old conservative US senator from Pennsylvania, perennial enemy of FDR & New Deal, & hopes I'll uncover some scandal about Pepper & embarrass his family & besmirch his memory, etc. I regret I can't find any smoking guns or stained sheets. I believe that Pepper's "affair" w/ Wilde must've been innocent & chaste — much as Oscar might've wished otherwise. One never knows of course. Pepper's tepid autobiog *Philadelphia Lawyer* (my copy cost 98¢), despite its sly title (a "Philadelphia lawyer" is slang for a shyster), predictably makes no mention of events at the Catskill Mountain House in September 1883. It presents a healthy sporty handsome WASP teen who, the very following year, while vacationing w/ family at Lake Minnewaska (which I can almost see from my kitchen window), was to fall in love with his future wife Charlotte & begin his career of monogamous hetero-philoprogenetivity. However, just to be perverse, let's comb the book for possible bits of unconscious camp.

> "Glory of youth glowed in his soul;
>   Where is that glory now?"
>
> — R.L. Stevenson

— Thus Pepper opens his memoir. His father died when he was five; George "hero-worshipped" his memory. His childhood summer home was called "Fairy Hill." His best friend was a "colored boy" named Willie Ryder.

"In later years vivid recollections" of playing in the streets of urban Philadelphia "quickened my interest in playgrounds & in the Boy Scout movement."

Young George loved light verse & musical comedy, especially Gilbert & Sullivan. No doubt like many Americans in 1882 and 3 he was already familiar with "Bunthorne" (a caricature of OW in *Patience*, with his poppy/lily/Picadilly/medieval hand, etc.) *before* meeting the real mccoy in the flesh. Pepper had himself acted in a children's production of *Pinafore* "in 1881 or thereabout."

The year after he met Oscar he enrolled in college where he proved popular & bright. A teacher "introduced me to Walt Whitman" — apparently not in the flesh, altho Walt was still alive & living nearby. Oscar himself met Walt in 1882 & (as already noted) kissed him, surely a great moment in Queer History. Mightn't it have been Oscar who first "introduced" Whitman to young George?

In college George perfomed as Dikaiopolis in a production of Aristophanes's *The Archarnians* & was photographed, looking very much as Oscar would no doubt have most liked to remember him, i.e., *Greek*. (See photograph.)

At that time "I had a pair of (pointed shoes) with dark green cloth tops in which I extravagantly rejoiced."

Along w/ Whitman he mentions other queer poets as favorites, incl. A.E. Housman — & altho he declared "I had rather be credited with some bits of light verse than awarded an LL.D.," nevertheless, "when lying awake at night I often recite (Milton's) *Lycidas* to myself, taking special delight in the catalogue of flowers culled 'to strew the laureate hearse where Lycid lies'."

The Peppers had converted from Quakerism to Episcopalianism before George was born. He remained a loyal & active chuchman all his life. "Order, form & color have always made to me a strong appeal. From my boyhood onward I found great satisfaction in the church services & especially in the service of Holy Communion…. For many years I served as an acolyte. I was responsive to the influence of church music but never had enough of a singing voice to be a member of the choir. For a number of years I was its librarian & sat vested in the stalls with the other boys."

In 1909 Pepper published a little work called *The Way: A Devotional Book for Boys*. I tracked down a used copy of this anodyne & soporific opuscule, hoping for hints of Pepper's hidden psychology — if any — & was rewarded with some dim lights:

✴   ✴   ✴   ✴

"The book is not intended for prigs or milk-sops. It is meant for the kind of boy who comes out for the team and who means to make an honorable place for himself in his school or college….

The author was a boy once. He cherishes the secret belief that he is a boy still. At all events, he has deep affection for the race, and he is eager to see the establishment of frank but reverent intercourse between them and Him who has chosen them to be His friends….

A boy understands what friendship is. He knows that among his companions there are a few in whose society he is always happy. He realizes that there is some unseen force which draws him toward them. No one who has ever felt this attraction will doubt the reality of Friendship. Like some other great realities of life, the thing is a mystery. As we grow older we learn by experience that there are many things in heaven and earth whose profound influence upon our lives we cannot fully explain. Friendship is one of these….

When you and your friend are together your natures mingle and you hold communion with one another, even if little talking is done. This communion is either a holy or an unholy communion. All depends upon whether the lower nature debases the higher, or whether the higher elevates and refines the lower. Doubtless you feel it easy to be truthful and pure and brave when you are with a certain friend. You say to yourself, "It seems impossible to be mean and low when I am with him." It is a help to you to grasp his hand and, as it were, to feel some of his strength flowing into yourself. Such a hand-grasp between friends is an outward and visible sign of an inward and spiritual grace given by the stronger to the weaker. This, you remember, is something like the definition of a sacrament....

The boy looks upon the man as stern and severe and unable to enter into the boy's thoughts. Suddenly something happens which opens the boy's eyes. He finds that the man loves him deeply, and can sympathize truly with him. Ever afterwards they are friends....You probably know another who regards the most sacred bodily functions as intended for mere self-gratification or as the subject of unclean jests and stories. Such a being is using his body as a mere toy of his passions. By so doing he loses all reverence for it; and when reverence is gone, he is ready to indulge in vulgar jokes about what is really sacred....

If you are still unstained, keep yourself pure. If the whiteness of your soul has been spotted, make the mightiest effort of your life to tear yourself away from whatever defiles....

If in a few days you are going to meet an older and a wiser friend, for whom you have deep affection and high respect, you find yourself wondering what he will think of you. You fear that you may have changed a little since the last meeting — that you have allowed your interest in his affairs to wane — that you have formed some habit of which he will not approve.

Almost unconsciously you use the days that remain as an opportunity to think more about him and his interests and to drive out of your mind and life whatever will make you uncongenial to him. Perhaps you write to him once or twice — telling him how eager you are to see him, and asking him to bring (it may be) some book of which you and he are fond, or reminding him of an interrupted conversation which you are anxious to resume.

As the days go by you find that the prospect of the meeting grows more and more delightful to you. At last the day of his arrival comes. You are actually in the presence of your friend. You are sure that you will never forget the happiness of the handshake and the joy of the greeting. There is an inspiration in his presence which makes of you a new creature. In later days you will look back to the communion as one of the turning-points in your life."

✳   ✳   ✳   ✳

I'm reminded of Mrs Gill, remember her?, and other unnamed guests at the Catskill Mt. House in Sept. 1883 who witnessed the little play produced by Pepper & his friend Oscar — the Mrs Gill who much later told Mrs Smith of the Greene Co. *Examiner* that they had remembered that magical evening all their lives. Of course Senator Pepper had to bury his memories of friendship with Oscar, who by 1895 had become the world's most notorious sodomite. But I doubt if Pepper *forgot* their friendship. I think it tinted (or tainted if you prefer) his later experience of friendship with boys — perhaps with one or more of the US Senate Page Corps lads shown in this snap from *Philadelphia Lawyer* (see photo).

(That's Pepper behind the bat, smoothing down his cowlick.) Again: I adduce no *evidence* of "impurity" — but then as any lawyer will tell you, absence of evidence proves exactly nothing.

The "Mary Powell" Steamboat

Press Release
"Oscar Wilde in the Catskills"
Vanishing Art #5
(Canto II of *riverpeople*)
July 1, 2010
(Feast of the Precious Blood)

"Heard By A Bird," By Sparrow —
"Oscar Wilde in the Catskills"

On August 18, 1882, Oscar Wilde added Phoenicia to the long list of American towns and cities where he lectured about the Aesthetic Movement — and wore aesthetic clothes. In Phoenicia he spoke at the Tremper House Hotel, a huge edifice on the Esopus vis-à-vis the railway station (i.e. on Plank Road). Wilde said he found the Catskills "charming"; and in fact he returned the next year (1883) to spend all of September in idleness at the famous Catskill Mountain House.

This column has learned that on August 18 of this year (2010), a group of "alternate" clergypeople will meet at an undisclosed spot in Phoenicia (perhaps in the woods where Tremper House once stood) to consecrate Oscar Wilde an official Saint & Martyr in their canonical doxologies. Sects and churches represented include the Moorish Orthodox Church of America, the Fatimid Order of Cairo, New York, the Circle of the Free Spirit (Independent Catholic Diocese of New York), the Esopus Druid Grove of the Universal Life Church of Modesto, California, and the Chapel of St. Anthony of Egypt (Non-Juring Anglican).

The conclave will declare that St. Oscar's Feast Day (his birthday, October 16) should be devoted to beauty, wine, poetry and love.

28 THE PHOENICIA TIMSS, JULY 1, 2010

Heard By A Bird
By Sparrow

"Shakespeare loves princes, and mistrusts kings."

— Alfred Harbage

Did you see the cloud shaped like a mandarin orange over Big Indian last Monday?

Oscar Wilde in the Catskills

On August 18, 1882, Oscar Wilde added Phoenicia to the long list of American towns and cities where he lectured about the Aesthetic Movement — and wore aesthetic clothes. In Phoenicia he spoke at the Tremper House Hotel, a huge edifice on the Esopus vis-à-vis the railway station (i.e. on Plank Road). Wilde said he found the Catskills "charming"; and in fact he returned the next year (1883) to spend all of September in idleness at the famous Catskill Mountain House.

This column has learned that on August 18 of this year (2010), a group of "alternate" clergypeople will meet at an undisclosed spot in Phoenicia (a perhaps in the woods where Tremper House once stood) to consecrate Oscar Wilde an official Saint & Martyr in their canonical doxologies. Sects and churches represented include the Moorish Orthodox Church of America, the Fatimid Order of Cairo, New York, The Circle of the Free Spirit (Independent Catholic Diocese of New York), the Esopus Druid Grove of the Universal Life Church of Modesto, California, and the Chapel of St. Anthony of Egypt (Non-Juring Anglican).

The conclave will declare that St. Oscar's Feast Day (his birthday, October 16) should be devoted to beauty, wine, poetry and love.

The above notice was published on July 1st, 2010 in the give-away fortnightly newspaper *The Phoenicia Times* (now defunct). The historical material on Oscar Wilde is of course 100% genuine (see Ellman's biog). The info about a coven of ecclesiastics canonizing St Oscar, however, refers not to a "real-life" event but to an ASTRAL CONVENTION — that is, to a convocation on the aetherial or imaginal plane, held between me and Bishop Mark Aelred Sullivan, Independent Catholic (Circle of the Free Spirit) of NYC, and others. Bishop Mark also prepared official canonization papers, which are included in the Documentation Box that accompanies this artwork.

On Aug. 18 (which also happens to be the date of the annual Welsh Bardic Festival & Competition), the anniversary of Oscar's visit to Phoenicia "will" occur as "foretold" by the poet Sparrow in his column in the *Phoenicia Times*, "Heard By A Bird," which consists largely of fake "village gossip" supposedly sent in by loyal readers but actually all written by Sparrow himself. (Note: See his excellent collected works, *America: A Prophecy: A Sparrow Reader*, published by Soft Skull Press.) In this case, however, the Oscar Wilde material was written by me and sent to Sparrow, along with a $5 bill as a "bribe" to publish the story. (In 1882 it would've been a *good* bribe.)

The publication of this material constitutes the artwork itelf, number 5 in the over-all series of Vanishing Art, and Canto II of the accompanying poem, *riverpeople*. I consider it "vanishing" because nothing could be more evanescent than a newspaper; moreover, by mentioning the now-overgrown site of the long-gone Tremper House Hotel, and by convening an astral moot there, I'm hoping to *spiritualize the landscape* for those

who read Sparrow's Column.

I've prepared several psychic map-collages and holy banners in connexion with this event, so at least some "traces" will remain and at some future date I may also organize an actual action in Phoenicia, similar to the others carried out or planned for the Esopus River Series — perhaps a celebration of St Oscar's Feast-day, with an offering to the River nymphs. The Oscar material may prove too rich for just one event.

For instance: As noted, in the following year Oscar returned to the Catskills and spent the whole month of September at the famous Catskill Mountain House, so often painted by artists of the Hudson River School. There Oscar met and befriended a 16-year-old boy from Philadelphia named George Pepper. Blond, handsome, athletic and mad about Gilbert & Sullivan, no doubt he was thrilled to meet the real "Bunthorne."

Pepper wrote a little musical comedy and Wilde helped him stage it (on the Veranda of the hotel) complete with a chorus-line of lads and lasses dressed in black and carrying sunflowers. I believe that not one of Oscar's official biographers has ever mentioned this little interlude. I got it from local history pamphlets and old newspapers in the Green Co. Archives. It strikes me as obvious that Oscar and Pepper were attracted to each other, although I imagine the relation remained chaste. A kiss or two, perhaps. Anyway — so I've written about it in *riverpeople*, Canto II, the text that accompanies the Esopus River Series of vanishing temporary landscape installations.

Oddly enough, George Pepper grew up to become the perennially re-elected US Senator from Pennyslvania, not only hyper-respectable but deeply conservative, indeed reactionary, and a great enemy of

FDR's New Deal. In his autobiog *Philadelphia Lawyer* the summer of 1883 is a blank. Pepper edited Oscar out of his life. However, he later also wrote a little tract for Episcopalian boys on "pure friendship" — and had himself photographed surrounded by cheerful Senate Pageboys….

Photos of young Pepper (in Greek costume) and old Sen. Pepper with his Pageboys, plus complete documentation of the "affair" with Wilde, plus pictures of hotels, railroads and steamships graced by Oscar's presence, are included in the Box of documents *in re:* "Oscar Wilde in the Catskills" — and also, some day (I hope) in the published version of *riverpeople,* my "long poem with history in it."

In "Oscar Wilde in the Catskills" the goal of re-enchanting the landscape becomes also an exercize in *queering the landscape.* In other words: there's something perverse and unnatural in the modern love of "nature", an artificiality that res-

onates with Classical pastorals and eclogues, as well as cetain proto-green strains of Late Romanticism.

And so what?

Is this "aestheticism" to be deemed a sin in terms of some PoMo theory of the Abject, or of the "Colonial Gaze"? Isn't it better to be *queer for nature* than queer for death, i.e., for the *antibios* of technopathocratic Kapitalismo? It may be impossible for us to become innocent and primitive — to bomb ourselves back to the Stone Age, so to speak — but not impossible to fall in love with the beauty of Earth as a sign of divinity. In fact, such a perverse act may turn out to be imperative.

For a secret sign we could wear green carnations.

Oscar Wilde said he found the Catskills "charming", and promised he'd return. We evoke him.

Canto III/1
Esopus Eclogue

        if wolves come back
to the Catskills I predict so will the
                        Wolf Clans
old geezer in bib overalls & rubber boots haranguing
the crowd in Kingston Bus Terminal Xmas morning:
                        "The horse & buggy days
are comin' back. Oil'll run out soon
                        — you fellers
(the ticket sellers)'ll be out of a job —
hope I live to see it"
                        then
                        "Happy Holidays"
he wished each of us individually & grandly
& vanished like a Hidden Prophet.

Among the Esopus the State had not yet emerged
all the stars were still visible
                        — the Principle of snow
                        — baroque excess
natura naturans — the original spectator sport —
every nerve fiber linked to some organ
of animate cosmos

Chas. Fourier (thinking of Tahiti, which had just been "discovered") preaches that Barbarism is infinitely preferable to Civilization & its "Black Turnips." Utopia ("Harmony") will be based on barbarities such as Horticulture & sexual license, not civilized agriculture, slavery & immiseration. *Harmony* will return to the Gift Economy of the barbarians, but on a higher gyre-level of undreamt luxuries & gastrosophic excess. Not Capt. Cook's Tahiti, so to speak, but that of Joseph Banks & the Romantics, or Gauguin or Melville — paradise regained.

Catskills as a vast Spiritualist *Summerland*
where everybody seems possessed by dead Indians
$600 shamanism weekends
                    Improved Order of Red Men
                         Boy Scout fantasies
unpaving the way for stately return of the Warranawongkong
with or without casino
from far-away Wisconsin Oklahoma Mexico
their lycanthropic polity of
                              unlegislated time
their "dead language" resurrected like
                         Cornish or Hebrew
          lost/found perceptual
                         consensus revived
wampum replaces money — beavers come back
all is forgiven — hemlocks come back
whispering like aeolian harps

Shamans often tell legends about Lost Books: — for instance: — "We once had a Book," the story begins, "in which all knowledge was included — But due to some supernatural cause or catastrophe the Book was withdrawn, taken back by the the Spirits, or else simply lost, & now we can no longer read."

Usually anthropologists explain this myth as shamanic chagrin at their embarrasing inferiority to "Whiteman's Magic" of literacy. But what if the stories were literally true — that all so-called Primitive societies were once upon a time *literate* — and therefore also the subjects of the State that literacy *always creates* (along w/ one or two other key technologies of hegemony such as irrigation & metallurgy) — and that one fine day these people, these fellahin, said fuck it — no more slaving for the King of Atlantis or whatever. Back to the Woods. Let's *revert* to hunting/gathering or swidden (slash'n'burn) economy — as in the Golden Age (i.e., the Paleolithic). Let's renounce literacy as the curse that brings civilization with it. No doubt it's a real treat for the ruling class — but an eternity of debt peonage & enforced ignorance for everyone else. Burn the Book & become post-literate — liberated from the text as spell or "fix"
     the hieroglyph-woven hypnotic web of
                         magic-at-a-distance
     that entices all the flies to the spider
     cannibal Pharaoh
               Moloch
                    Mammon
     pale Galilean — Marduk — St Paul
     Babylonian Papism or
                         Free Market economy
               "Sorry, boss — no comprende —
               we're hopelessly illiterate
               completely unemployable

riverpeople

neo-noble
enfants sauvages"*

The beaver in fact is already back — along with the raptors (eagles, red hawks, turkey vultures…) as well as bears, coyotes, & a zillion deer. NY State was 40% forested in 1900, now 90% — as scrubwoods take over ruined farms, abandoned factories, dry canals
Soon the wolves
will
let the oil run out
let the asphalt rot
let impudent mushrooms & vigorous chicory
crack thru macadam like Max Ernst
in a frenzy of frottage & decalcomania

& given that we shall once again be eating "our relatives" red deer canada geese woodchucks rabbits racoons eels squirrels wild turkey ducks shad beavers & bear
why not
once more
dress in their skins
& think with them
become them —
receive their powers
w/ terrified gratitude.

* Thanx & tip-o-th-fez to anarcho-anthropologist James C. Scott of Yale for this scenario.

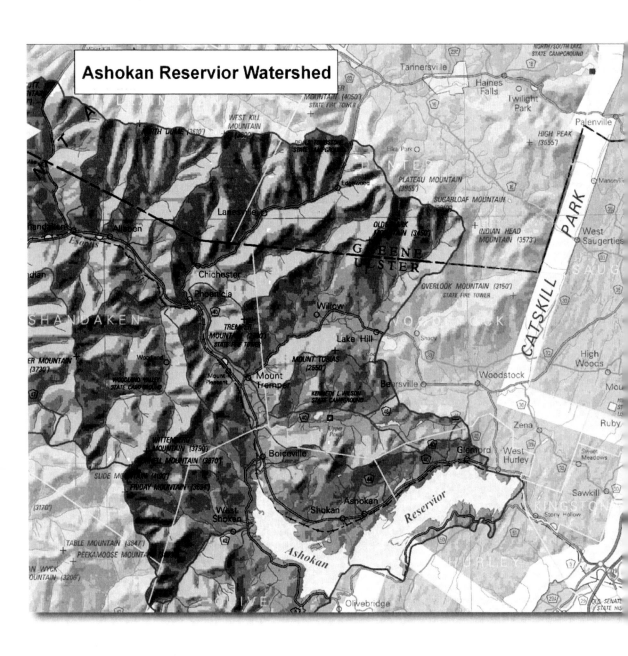

Canto III/2
The Ashokan Dam Allegorized
As the Rape of Aegina Daughter of Esopus
By Zeus in the Form of the U.S. Eagle

i.

the ghost of Malthus admits OK
    I was wrong — it isn't "resources"
                    that run out
it's the *imaginaire* the
             shared space of night.
Usura defines us
    by taking a cut of our very
                 insubstantiality
from the *duende* itself the
             Gipsy cards
slices of our luck
             slices of our livers
like kebabs on a spit as Hafez sez.
There's not enough to *go around* anymore
it's spread *too thin* it's been
             monopolized
                televangelized &
                   downsized
to a *fare-thee-well*
        an Ashokan Farewell.

ii.

Malthus goes on
        Now that I'm dead myself
I see the dead hand of the police
on the thigh of Nature

63

        Flora
        Ceres
        Ops
        Aegina
        Pomona
            & "Old Night"

    the sexuality of the Dead
        all of it marked BANK OF HADES
            smallest denominations 10 billion dollars*
iii.

Ashokan Farewell
seventeen villages drowned to their steeples
but every last grave dug up & moved
                            to dry land
lest godforbid some rich Manhattanite shld
someday inadvertently drink eau de bones
                    or shower in ectoplasm.**

---

* Last time I visited my favorite Taoist supplies shop on Mott St I noticed that the Bureaucrats of Hell are apparently nowadays accepting crude facsimile counterfeits of US currency — $100 bills — and it was definitely a *Cassandra Moment:* — money hasn't "gone to heaven" as my old friend millionaire Gordon used to say — but straight to HELL.

** Q: — Who invented soda water?
Answ: — Joseph Priestly, radical theologian & champion of Phlogiston Theory — fled murderous reactionary English mob (who burned down his house & lab) to Northumberland, Pennsylvania, in 1794 — a Pantisocratic nucleus — but Coleridge & Southey finked out & never emigrated. Seltzer (from the German spa Neider-Selters) was naturally carbonated — Priestley synthesized it via neo-hermetic alchemy — refused to take out a patent, so all humans could benefit freely from its digestive magic: Pneumatic Theory — the Romantic Science *par excellence*. Tip-o-fez to Mike Jay's *Atmosphere of Heaven*.

iv.

Aptly named THE WATER AUTHORITY
like some Gnostic Aeon who's usurped
      the realm of the Undines
lunar mercurial ordered chaos of
          Leonardo's Notebooks
chopped & diced like so many carrots & onions
beneath the guillotine of Pure Reason.
G-d Himself forbids counting — tells King David
not to take a census — counting is bad luck
Romano-Herodian tyranny — sin against
          divine vagueness
measurement is oppression. Can you imagine
a neo-Pythagorean Mazdean & even
        non-numeric
        mathēma?
including aquamancy dowsing baptizing
        anthroposophical hydrotherapy
        rectified Mesmerism
        Paracelsan chaotic
          attractors
        & oceans of lemonade?

v.

FORMER SITE OF SHOKAN
now sunk beneath waves like the
        drowned City of Ys
a yokel Atlantis a local Hy Bresil
sink-hole of resentment & impotent
        muttering
monument to futility invisible except
        in parching droughts
when (so they say) ghost-blue nite-lights
glow beneath the stygian muck
where some nameless dorf was disappeared
on the altar of Chase Manhattan Bank
      & its Illuminati Water Lords
decked out like Aztecs in frockcoats of
        human skin
top hats & spats keeping watch by night
for boogyman Islamist terrorists carrying
        sacks of LSD

creeping up in miniature Japanese
                              kamikaze submarines*
or rapelling down on ropes from hot air balloons
                    w/ scimitars & box-cutters in their teeth.

vi.
(Nonnos, *Dionysiaca*, VII, 210 ff.)

Juppiter now deceitfully changes form
on heat before season into an eagle
overflying Esopus River beady-eyeing
the Rivergod's daughter Aegina like
an omen of wingèd rapture. Plummets
from sky & zooms in over riverbank
scoping out slick naked body
                              wet hair
not satisfied w/ far-seeing he
yearns for a close-up of
                              sleek whiteness
even tho he could easily send his All-Seeing Eye
(& what an I) circumnavigating the cosmos
round the bounds of infinity if he wished
yet thinks it not good enough to glut his
scopophile lust for just one virgin girl.

vii.
(Nonnos, cont.)

Can this fizz be Saturn's genitals again
as if foam itself had a mind
& shaped water into selfperfected birth
a neo-Aphrodite water-born of river's
                    self-pregnant waves?
I spy silverfoot stretched beneath
                              stream's race
a Moon on her wet way to insomniac
                              Endymion's
                                   couch
white as the snows of heaven —
                    so spake some voice
from beneath the swirling eddys
                    of Esopus.
Zeus voyeured the swimming girl Aegina

---

* Used to be one on display at Mystic Seaport Maritime Museum in Connecticut. Children
   adored it.

surveyed her naked breasts & all
her flesh except the secrets of her lap
(modest god!) — his mind crept down
      from heaven
toward that blue pool pricked on
     by Cupid's dart —
little boy vs. shaggy Lord of Thunder
lightningbolts vs. toy arrows.
He carries her off in his talons.

viii.
(Nonnos, op. cit., XXIII, 284 ff.)

Esopus witnesses the rape & chases after
cursing like Oceanus to Tethys
Nay I will set all my waters
against the lightnings of Olympus
drown the sun in my quenching blood
put out the stars of heaven —
under the Bear I'll wash the axles
     of the Wain
celestial Nile I'll drag down from
     its milky path
& give it a new home in some
     Celtic Thule
Tethys awake! I'll swallow Capricorn
& piss on Aquarius!

ix.
(*ibid.*, VII, 252 ff)

As he flies/flees upward w/ the naiad
Juppiter lets loose a fiery spark
like a stalk of fennel (which will
burst into flame if you hold it
    up to the sun —
so combustible it conceives a little flame &
    gives birth to woodborn fire)
& tossed it in the stream.
     At once
the River burst into flame as if
    turned to petroleum
boiled up against its banks w/

                        clouds of smoke
from incinerated waterlilies shrivelling
                                galingale
crisped rushes reek of soot curling
whirling in circles to intoxicate the very
                        heavenly vaults
fish hid in mud — slime kindled and broiled
as the spark ran under water in
                        deep channels
poured forth polluted steam.

x.
(*ibid.*)
                        Hydriads
                        & Undines
driven naked from subaqueous dens
swift barefoot & unveiled fled
burning like Vietnamese monks, dived
unveiled into whatever puddle would
                                take them.
From now on ESOPUS goes lame in
                                one leg
& limps like a gimp or Fisher King.
Wounded by dams & reservoirs he
                lurches like Long John Silver
                        toward Saugerties
wounded vet of the war against that
one-dollar eagle that Nobodaddy
the Water Authority the Highway Authority
the Conscousness Authority despoiler of rivers
                        & their organic nymphs.

xi.
(ibid., XIII, 201 ff.)

Aegina meanwhile abandoned pregnant
unwed teen mother languishes on desert isle
                                off Boeotia
(we cld think of it as Esopus Island in the Hudson)
gives birth to a boy she names Aeacus
then somehow disappears leaving him all
robinson-crusoe'd & alone w/ no playmates
but a nest of ants

busyfooted earthcrawlers
he prays to his absent father to
                    metamorphose them
from clay-born aphasic
              insignificant bugs
to an armed host of mortals w/ speech
the MYRMIDONS the prototype fascist police
Aeacus becomes their warlord & leads them
carrying a wellwrought shield showing a sham bird
rapting up a naked girl
                a rivergod on fire
Aegina mourning her father
                    morose & depressed
mourning for stiff-knee'd crippled Esopus.*

xii.
Novo Ordo Seclorum

13 bolts in one claw & bearing on its breast the
      Washington family coat-of-arms (stars'n'stripes)
(unless it's actually meant to be Adam Weishaupt
            who founded the Illuminati in 1776…)
He Approves The Undertaking
                annuit coeptis
of a 13-storied ziggurat surmounted
by the Eyeball of Total Surveillance
            the Rhizomatic pan-Panopticon
            the Global Accident

---

* Classicist & poet Charles Stein alerted me to the fact that Aeacus (son of Zeus & Aegina) is
   the father of Peleus, who is the father (by the sea-nymph Thetis) of the hero Achilles.
   Achilles inherits the Myrmidons as personal bodyguards; moreover, he is associated in the
   Iliad with the motif of a burning river (see Book XXI; probably the source for Nonnos. See
   also *Apollodorus' Library & Hyginus' Fabulae, Two Handbooks of Greek Mythology,* trans. Smith &
   Trzaskoma, index under "Asopus" and "Peleus.") Of course, if Zeus had raped Thetis, as
   he intended, she would have given birth to a son destined to avenge all the suffering of the
   "House of Esopus" by killing Zeus & becoming the next King of Heaven! Luckily for Juppiter, Prometheus warned him of this prophecy in time. Not only did Zeus spare Thetis his
   "favors," he also freed Prometheus in gratitude, after 30,000 years of liver-plucking torture.
   Perhaps the image of FIREWATER here symbolizes (as in alchemy) a kind of divinization of
   matter. This symbolism could be either positive, as with Dionysus & his "invention" of
   wine, a kind of fire-water; or negatively, as with the River Esopus, who becomes fire-water
   to his detriment. But *both* these motifs have both positive and negative aspects. Fire-water
   is a kind of poison, as the American Indians learned (esp. after the alchemists' secret of distillation was profaned); whereas Esopus can say, like Nietzsche, whatever doesn't kill him
   makes him stronger. (Lumps of coal are still being taken out of the Greek Asopus River to
   this very day.)

the Internet
In God We Trust — because we've given up
pretending to believe in Gold
                    (thanx to the great anti-alchemist
                    Nixon who transmuted gold into sheer
                    nothingness — pure imagination —
                    pure debt —
                              pure shit)

Behold this hieroglyphic amulet of the
only magic that ever really
worked — money.
    Note the microscopic owl of
Athena

(upper righthand shield on recto —

upper righthand indentation —
                              use
powerful magnifying glass)
    & note Genghiz Khan's arrows
    in the eagle's claw.

    xiii.

Heraldry functions as a branch of esoteric hermeneutics
as used by Gérard de Nerval,
Alfred Jarry & other
                              proto-surrealists &
              'pataphysicians
links the shield of the Myrmidons &
the Great (Reverse) Seal of the U.S. Buck as understood
by Nicholas Roerich the guru who convinced
his disciple Henry Wallace to wheedle
FDR into redesigning the Yankee Dollar
with Freemasonic-designed Eye-in-Pyramid
potent ju-ju. Roerich was probably a
                    Russian spy
or agent of Shambhala or tool of the
                         Illuminati
I lived near his memorial museum on W. 107th St
for years & learned the whole saga
              from its gossipy tell-all librarian.

xiv.

Just as the Esopus Indians were
exterminated (but not quite) by the Dutch
in the role of Zeus so the Esopus River
was lamed by lightningbolt technopathocracy
of dams & stolen watersheds. The
next war will not be for oil
                                    but water
                                            they say
imperialism is thirsty work
                    Capitalism wants to own the
                                    Four Elements
"sell water by the river bank"
sell Earth & the Fire of heaven
sell air —
                    usura
            lames the rivers
                            rapes the nymphs
money itself is pollution
                    "The Devil's Shit"*

* On the other hand
                    there's something to be said
for living in the feudal realm
                    of NYC's watershed
paternalist protection from
                    development's fracking ravages
heavy industry or biochemical
                    savages.
In return we tug our forelocks
                    & admire the preservationism
of Nature as image of itself down here
                    on the Arts Reservation.

Eight-foot Conduit Used to Divert Esopus Creek at Dam Site

Canto III/3
Ashokan Dam & Reservoir

"It was like the end of the world"
                              — whitehaired ex-teamster
observers had seen a church steeple
rising from ebbing drought waters
                              like return of Atlantis
City surveyors cut down mother's prize roses
a blind miller lived there could tell
                 the color of a horse by touch
chief engineer
rode stately horses liked cockfights
                              Italian limosines
                 $13000 big cigars
wildcat strike for 5¢ raise supported by IWW
brass checks
only redeemable at the Company Store
                              5000 loaves a day
"chariot race" of 3-mule teams their black
drivers standing up cracking long whips
                              whooping & waving

                 "10000 unskilled wild desperate dumped
                 suddenly havoc 1907 roaring camp
                 echoed drunken songs seethed banditry
                 outlawry murder brawls orgies
                                             stole away
                 rob pillage isolate farms ten
                 bloody years of their lives"
                              (signed) Sgt Carmody
                              Board of Water Supply Police
1909 cut wife's throat with a knife
                 "a low breed of aliens"
laudanum 10¢ a bottle at local stores
"even the dead will not be permitted to rest"
40 cemetaries — headstone cracked in 3 places
decided to rescue the jewels from her grave

corpse sat up & shrieked
        gnawed by huge teeth of prehistoric beavers
riding on a big black horse
              "torn at his heart strings"
25 years of litigation, lawyers "shook the plum tree"
        West Hurley
        Glenford
        Ashton
        Olive Branch
        Brown's Station
        Olivebridge
        Olive City
        Brodhead's Bridge
        Shokan
        W. Shokan
        Boiceville
all gone under
represented by windbag lawyer Alonzo Clearwater
about whom I could write a whole book
                  (but who'd care)
70 year old Emma Cudney of Shokan
owned the largest ginseng plantation hereabouts
$6–$7 per lb. in China 1909
            Mr Ghallager fiddled
            at dances $3–$5 "I had
            a horse of my own they
            fed me wherever I went"
covered bridge at Bishop's Falls floated
off its moorings crashed into the Dam
Halley's Comet to the SE over South Mt.
Sad & empty marched thru the territory
last St Patrick's Day Ball at Pythian Hall
                blotted out
                  until now

the last hold-out Oranzo Giles
"astrologer" —
           let's name our
Society after him
        The ORANZO GILES Memorial
           Neo-Luddite Militia
              & Chowder Soc.
first transcontinental flight 1909
Ford Co. adopts assembly line 1913
spirit of efficiency & productiveness
plugging the dam. "Home" lost forever.

87 mules burned to death
        began to look like a ghost town
arrested & fined heavily for "innocent trespassing"
Water Supply Police an invading occupying force
poaching is not uncommon.*

The Naturalist John Burroughs Tours the New Ashokan Dam

* Thanx to *Last of the Hand-Made Dams* for many quotes, and to Jay & Molly.

ADDENDA

1. Geologist Yngvar Isachsen has devoted decades to proving that the strange circular course of the upper Esopus results from a huge meteor (or comet) impact centered on Panther Mt., which occurred "aeons ago," long before the dinosaurs. The object must have been over a third of a mile in diameter and would have exploded like "eleven trillion tons of dynamite." (See *Discovery* magazine, Aug. 2000.)

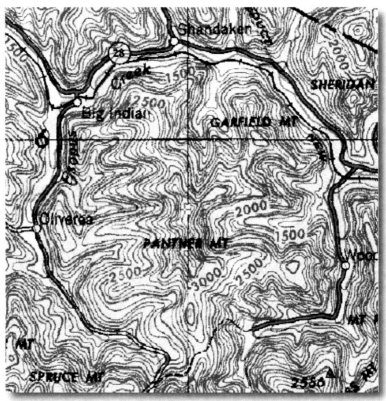

The Upper Esopus "Rosette" Encircling Panther Mountain

2. In 1896 William Jennings Bryan, running for President as a Democrat ("cross of gold" and all that) visited Lake Winnisook at the source of the Esopus, and was greeted by huge crowds. Bryan of course ruined the Populist cause by involving it in national politics, and he was a bit of a fool; however, I believe he deserves some sympathy for his principled stand against evolutionary theory in the Scopes Trial, not because he was a Christian (lots of leftist Populists and rural socialists were Xtian in those days, strange as it may now seem to modern liberals) — but becuse he opposed Social Darwinism as a crypto-ideological scam to bolster Capitalist greed and racism — which it *was* (and still *is*). For this reason I include him amongst the "heroes" of *riverpeople*.

Canto IV/1
Some Swimming Holes

i.

Tongore Rd

Probably there was no such Indian as Chief Tongore
on the one hand but on the other hand
                                    maybe there was.
Tongore Road says the guitar
                        where Esopus spurts
from Ashokan captivity tumbles down to fertile
flatland *tres riches* marshes no longer rushes
but imbues itself into bucolic
boon to horticulturalists & duckhunters
wolf turkey tortoise crow.

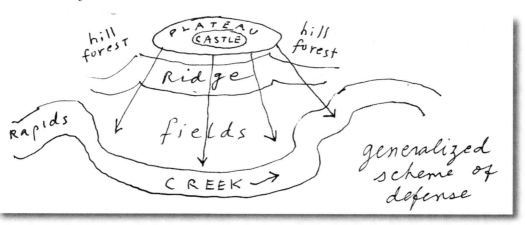

1. strategic

2. oeconomic
Immediate access to hunting/gathering river & marsh as well as uplands for winter
hunting (such as deer). Frequently flooded fields' renewed fertility means you can do
gardening without having to move the whole village every few years.

3. spiritual

Similar aesthetics inform the siting of holy shrines in Persia & China, megalithic sites in Ireland & Effigy Mound sites in Wisconsin, but the Esopus "castles" were not monuments or graveyards but miniature biospheres — microcosms.

Tongore Rd — same precise concept. Tongore Town Park legal swimming hole on the Esopus — former Indian cornfield is now beach. This was Wyltmeet Castle — where the *wild ones met* — today a row of old country houses occupies the razorback ridge where the Castle once stood, wooded palisade surrounding peaceful wigwams, very like a dragon line in feng shui — a power spot as Don Juan Castañeda would say especially on the coldest day of the year when we went searching for it — like the Ice Giant legends collected amongst the Munsee, or the Micmac (compared by Charles Leland to Norse mythology) (suggesting pre-historic circum-polar circum-arctic cultural matrix — a notion I find plausible — but then — I'm still holding out a sliver of hope for the *Walum Olum* as genuine "Delaware" lost holy book...) Frost spirits in a state of high glee —splashing around in boisterous streams the color of frozen daiquiris with extra ice from the deep heart of the ICE — pale emerald. Tanked on ozone.

Canto IV/2
The Bee

The quilting bee shows that agrarian anarcho-social will to power can vie with any
Pygmy Music or Turkish Radio

epiphany

on museumized Sundays here in the twilight of

anonymity

1. voluntary attractive labor
2. free chicken feathers
3. free recycled trash old dresses
   drapes remnants — thriftcraft
4. conviviality — group afflatus
   Deep Gossip. Wit. Social (auto)poiesis
   Poetry of the Hands
5. festivity. Coffee & cake
   plus
   what other stimulants in those days when
   laudanum was 10¢ a bottle at the country store
   & Granny was an herbalist. Good quilts
   are psychedelic as any Persian carpet.
6. Individuals can become masters, i.e., recognized
   artists w. unique voices — but always with
   some medieval traces of anonymity, of & by
   the Bee
   its temporary communitas social symbolic warmth.
7. Economy of the Gift: a good quilt isn't meant to
   be sold but given at a wedding or other potlatch
   then handed down mother to daughter etc.

The BEE has male counterpart — one-day barn raisings
w/ fiddler & beer
works of art
often far more beautiful than their own farmhouses
elemental zen
farmers imagine the inner lives of animals
with Imaginal *anima* that treats
each Sun-red sun-lit dung-dark stable

architecturally as a potential Bethlehem.
                              Quilts & barns
alike are charged with thick eros
    therefore protected with magic hex sign
                              or mystic mandal*
                              patterns that uncannily
predict strange attractors of complexity theory
signs older than writing — one of many
                              origins of the alphabet
talismans of linkage & blockage
hypnagogic meanings without content
                     or with too much content
                              for conscious parsing
like the deeds of Hermes as an infant.

Scraps & remnants of old texts & maps
intricately arranged as spirit snares
fly paper for fairies baited animated w/
                              images & sijils
                              honey traps
to seduce — sacrifices to placate —
burnt offerings to attract *djinn*
salamanders created of pure fire

if you slept under such a coverlet you'd
dream veridical dreams like Ibn Sereen
            including all the "Chinese Numbers"
                              like rooster equals 38
sewing machine palmtree umbrella knife
generate random algorithms that might
                              perturb the aether
free jazz à la Sun Ra that might spontaneously
                              re-order the universe
or nudge a pair of dice toward sevenness

                              cut from paisley or calico
arranged lozenge-wise in archaic sunbursts
could be
            Esopus Indian arrowheads
            tantrik vajras
            crystals
            amber beads (w/ petrified bugs)

* I prefer the Persian form of this old word meaning magic circle cf. Latin or Etruscan *mundus,*
  pit or mound as *axis mundi,* world-axle.

        lodestones bristling w/
                magnetized nails &
                iron filings
you see displayed a series of magic lantern scenes
                as if on silken screens
each one representing the secret ritual
of some local 19th century fraternal or sororal
                  order
in the great rogue masonic conspiracy to
            re-paganize monotheism

                              — viz:

the Society of Ancient Druids of Newburgh NY — circa
1799 — originally revived by John Toland (founder of Pantheism) & passed down to Wm Blake who initiated Thomas
Paine who initiated blind preacher Elihu Palmer who initiated his disciples at the Druid's Head Tavern in Manhattan,
some of whom had a Temple of Nature upriver in Newburgh
— wiped out or driven underground by the Illuminati Panic

John Toland

Black Shriners — founded at Chicago World's Fair by
Ottoman Grand Orient Bektashi-Dunmeh shaykhs —
heretical Islam of the Janissaries & followers of False Messiah Sabbatai Sevi — fezzes — crescent moons & pyramids,
sacramental wine & haschisch

Improved Order of Red Men
attempt to appropriate & preempt
the magic power of the defeated
power of the alien forest
              native herbs &
                local genies
erase guilt by disguising oneself
in the flayed victim's skin
              paradoxical result
                of bourgeois alienation
one becomes the enemy
            — race traitor
              — prisoner of love

the Grange (Order of Husbandry)
founded 1876 in Fredonia NY way out in
                    Chautauqua Co.
by Upstate apple farmers w/ Celtic names
revived & still today celebrates the RITES OF ELEUSIS
which they inherited from an Italian Prince in Naples

where the secret'd been secretly preserved since
6th century AD & eventually incorporated into Masonry
like every mystery cult & pagan survival
now to become mytho-ideology for agrarian
                              Cooperative Populism
Pomona Flora Ceres incarnate as farmwives
maiden wife crone

and I invite you spirits & humans to a ritual in my head
Moorish Orthodox Non-Juring Anglican
                    Bengali Tantra Oveyssi Sufi
                                   Shiite extremist
Rosy Cross Rosy Crescent Rosy Yin-Yang
Hermetic Santeria in which Xtian saints
are syncretized w/ Greco-Roman Egyptian
Celtic Norse Mesopotamian Hindu Taoist
African AmerIndian Atlantaean pantheons
                    Emperor Akbar's *Din Ilahi*
universalism carried to delirious extremes
but outwardly pure High Church
Anglo-Catholic smells bells &
                    Social Gospel
w/ a weekend retreat center former
                    Catskill summer camp
                         now secret monastery
                             rustic cabins
wafts of myrrh in the cloudy
                    rainsodden cedars
Sung Dynasty misty Catskills "Cold Mountain"
w/ giant hemlocks surrounded by
islands of plush moss
    intoxicated on ozone of waterfalls
& luminous fungus of Mao Shan.

Why Christianity you ask?
Ans. — because the land has been
            Xtianized for 500 years
                    local djinn must be
                         propitiated
our own Xtian ancestors must be propitiated
meaning the ghosts in our nerves & blood
not to mention the unmentionable
total entanglement of Anglican libido
chained to childhood reveries
    black garments w/ too many buttons

lace surplices
            starch &
                  beeswax
that 15th century German limewood statuette
of St John Baptist as an adolescent
            nearly naked — lamb — crook
                  honey & locusts
                        same color as the wood
the Universal Life Church of Modesto, California
I've been a member for decades, teaches
St John the B. was the true secret messiah
also believed by the Mandean Gnostics of Mesopotamia
& by certain circles w/in Templar Masonry
"head of Baphomet"
            his grotto
                  his skin desert rosewood
                        Beardsley's Salomé
Flaubert's St Anthony
         St Anthony of Egypt patron saint
of LSD & "workers in hemp"
            Secret Gospel of Mark
            Jesus in the *Egyptian Magical Papyri*

St. Anthony of Egypt

& then suddenly I thought: Jesus
the failed messiah — the False Messiah
just like Sabbatai Sevi — never
rose from the Dead & certainly never
Came Again "while some of ye yet live"
failed to convert the Jews
      failed to found a religion
                  based on his actual
                        theories
and what if failure is the
                  last possible Outside
Failure the sole refuge from
                  Capitalist heaven
"His" failure to redeem our sins
            would leave us
                  pure antinomians

poetry — sacred because it's such an
                        utter failure
poverty deviance crime helpless passion
                  madness all sacred
because totally futile — no

monetary value —
price
maybe Jesus escaped to India & became a fakir
or to Celtic Britain w/ the Holy Grail
why not — Sabbatai died in bed — and
if 'He' was crucified then that too was
a failure
Jesus a kind of Simon Magus or
charlatan
flawed magus
such a zero point would be
itself
hugely sacred
this despised pervert Jesus
apostate agitator of rabble
convert to Islam. Dead Jesus.
Conceptual loophole
into other possible dimensions —
non-Euclidean spaces
invisibility perhaps.
Jesus the queer mushroom

Sabbatai Sevi?

Jesus the terrorist.
The wash-out. The Con. The Pretender.
Cagliostro. Secretly married w/ 8 kids.
Secretly with Lazarus in the Turkish Bath.
Secretly w/ Judas. And yet
simultaneously
divine
as any orisha drunk on rum & cigars
"I am the Truth" & the Truth is
unnatural
ambiguous subaqueous distorted baroque pearl
god as failure — god as paedophile priest
god as burglar exile pimp etc.
yet the Infant of Prague forever
spangled w/ seed pearls in his
kafkaesque grotto
aha
now I get it
this makes perfect sense
this completes the quilt
(imagine I'm three old ladies
with scissors)

imagine yourself flinging this
                                    very big quilt
across a huge feather bed
                stretching out over a whole
                                landscape of linen-white
                                                            snow
in patterns of ice lace & living crystal
                                        — a quilt
as big as a county w/ all its
                    kills vlys hollows
                                    mountains & dales
blue nerves as rivers green patches
as neo-pastoral autonomous zones
                        a map as big as the
                                        territory it represents
one inch equals one inch
                    every angle squatted by angels.

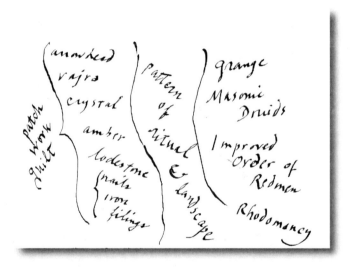

DREAM MESSAGE FROM PLANTS

"Civilization IS its discontents
throw away yr seratonin uptake inhibitors
like crutches at Lourdes & dare
to conceptualize the death of shopping"

Ice Harvesting In The 1870s

In the foreground, next to open water, is a wooden chute used as a pathway
for large blocks of ice. The ladderlike device is an A-frame used to hold a pulley.
Ropes keep it vertical or at another desired angle. A rope through the pulley
attaches to a set of tongs used to lift the blocks of ice.
[Photos from the Haber collection, *Esopus,* edited by Karl R. and Susan B. Wick]

Canto IV/3
The Natural Ice Trade

I still say "ice box"
its musty under-tray of meltwater
rotary fan in spidery frame
                 ommmmmmmmmm
to catch every
        wisp of chill escaping from
               white enamel mummy-case
& waft it round the afternoon
            kitchen
               forever.

Children naturally admire those who
             work w/ Elementals
Ice, Fire, Oceanus, Space, Farmer Brown
electric trolley men like tropical eels
exude ambiguous sexuality — so
children ran after ice wagons that
    jogged & wobbled over cobble-stones — ice
        menhirs shifted — showers of
           vajras spangled
              the asphalt
we plucked them up like lingams
        of manna & sucked them
a disgrace to public hygiene & health
like most of childhood's epicurean tastes.

Contrary to myth "Marco Polo" couldn't've
brought back secret of ice-cream to Italy
from "China" because the Chinese
            are lactose-intolerant
don't care for milk products — q.e.d. The Silk Road
passes thru Persia however & those Aryan cowboys
              claim ice-cream
clotted cream & archaic rose-water even today
        old Tehran hands will remember

Persian alchemists playing around with ice & fire
like cinnabar.
          The secret of ice-cream
is of course rock salt — only a Hermeticist
would've thought of such a paradox — how
diamondlike rock displays the Signature of water
                         congealed to ice
& will therefore transform mercuric fluid
                to pure crystal
        in the Hermetic vessel

Neo-Luddism doesn't abandon us
    to suffocating Augusts of
        Bengal-on-the-Hudson
            w/out tinkling lemonade
                or popsicles
Farmer Brown has an *ice house*
his triple-X moonshine applejack is
           on the rocks
we'll sit out on the porch
after the ball is over
after the Yuppie Rapture in 2012 AD
on the Phalanstery veranda in our
             deck chairs
w/ palmetto fans & afternoon absinthes
               in either hand
like luxury Catskill Mountain hotel circa 1883
                  but for free
gastrosophic Pantagruelism
         Thelemite Pantisocracy
            permanent holiday
"Attractive Labor" "Museum Orgies" "Phalanstery Operas"
communication by dove
           or telepathy
HARMONIAL humans will grow tails
w/ hands at the tips & an eye in
           the palm of that hand
the famous *Archibras* after which
    the Surrealists named their house organ
ice-swans for banquets & huge
blocks for ice sculpture — ice palaces
built every winter in Central Park
    illuminated with fireworks
our sleighs à la Russe heaped up

w/ illegal furs
gogolian troikas chased by
Catskill neo-wolves
whizz thru balsamic forests like
Winter Queens in a Rosicrucian ballad
lit by fateful Moon…

Natural Ice
   "He's a Natural Ice tycoon"
made a million
   soothing the brows of Antillian
                  pirates & orphans
Natural Ice a principle of Health
   star-beamed from Polaris
      in Ursa like the
pure Illuminati seven-step Astral Shuffle
of dream yoga in the Shawangunk Ice Cave of
   Shiva's holy popsicle.
                  Ice Queens.
                        Ice freaks. They
do it in the snow.
         Inside the Sno-Globe paperweight
in some Austrian Amanita muscaria moment of
amor fati you must repeat the same
fetishistic ritual — transformation
into wolf or bear or crow in non-stop ecstasy
   for a large slice of eternity:
                  DEVA-LOKA.
         Icy slushy sperm of Shiva
      lightning cream of Indra
   Soma vajra dew —
            natural

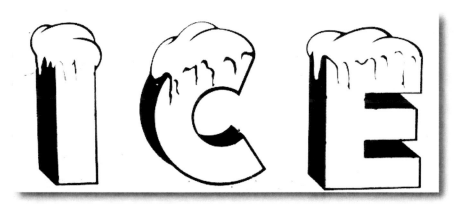

Thomas Eakins, Study For "The Swimming Hole"

Canto IV/4
Swimming Hole at Undisclosed Location

escaping from Ashokan
                  Reservoir's dead hand
Aegina stages her titanic break-out
                      at Spillway Channel
one Sun Day in January with frozen
                    Wagnerian chaodes
hurls herself toward West Hurley
               in a diamond spritz of
                          bitter bergs.
Meanwhile Asopus himself oozes
                    southeast
              to meet her
                  in Pacama
down together to the hamlet of Tongore
                    & its public beach
where Catskill trout-stream becomes sluggish farm
                          valley river
elbowing & ox-bowing its dark sweet mud
onto Esopus Indian cornfields & 12 generations
of double Dutch big farmers.
                    On the left bank
the steep long cliff wall of Hurley Mt
on the right a fat riverbedland
                of sleepy crops
& illegal Mexican farmworkers.
                      Up in the hills at
                        Eagle's Nest
they say a Juke-like remnant of
recalcitrant inbred recluse hicks is
                still holding out.
One summer day a decade ago when weather
replicated Singapore
                my dope dealer "Doctor" K
& I drove forth in search of swimming holes
following rumor

between fields of nameless crops &
                              pre-fab barns
                                        baking in place
till the road dipt into a shallow bourne
for lambs or cows (but now there are none)
arched over druid-grove-wise with
                              sentient somnolent green
backed up to a natural organic dam or damlet
a deepish placid umber amber pool appeared
with the eco-logic of theocratical eclogue
                    like a cool summer soup
                              of broth & riverweed.
Breaking out our beverage cooler & zigzags
we waded & floated buddhistically
                              fever-free amphibians
toe-ing the silty muck & imagining
two pallid giggling farmgirl avatars of the
                              local Undines
or perhaps they were real.
                         Every topos
                              has its eros
                                   or erotes
but some are more equal than others
w/ unfair shares of feng shui
                              trembling veils
bezels for bucolic
sex with Elementals — invisible but tangible
odoriferous &/or semi-audible
not quite present
                         maybe just stepped out
maybe not yet born
                         but pregnant
with some adolescent Triton or Naiad —
No Ideas but in Persons
                         as Corbin put it —
personal — sexual — hence political.
Is there a politics of swimming holes?
Ask the poor suckers of High Falls
who thought the People owned the local hole
— but — turned out the Volunteer Fire Dept.
                              held the deed
surreptitiously sold it to a good-old-boy local developer
for a measly 60 grand — *fait accompli* —
public swimming hole? Sounds like
                    Socialism to us, pal.

Meanwhile we're turning toad
like Cheech & Chong
    only our eyes above water
           tongues growing longer
skin all warty clammy & green
               dreaming of August moonlight
                  skinnydippings for
                     10,000 years
thinking the same long thought
    from Algonkian Arcadia to nude Jukes
            lost to all sense of sin
blond freshwater porpoises
       lunar gooseflesh'd
             temporary
                were-frogs
Virgilian secret ritual
       uninnocent nymphs
         & feral fauns —
           neo-Kallikaks.
Undinism
      underwater in
            public ponds or
              municipal pools
for kicks: — Mer-Sex: — a
        whole water-scape's
slow unconscious rape — like
      creaming on a sleeper beside you
                 in the river bed.
Frog-spawn. The feel of slithery eel
          on bare feet.
Dappled with sun-slant like an
        all-green kaleidoscope.
Emerald subaqueous OZ with a
        periscope of jade.
Get Down With Slime.
       Subliminality.
       Submersion.
Undinic consciousness as waking dream.
Human body already 90% H_2O
        with residual minerals
           silver & gold
— why not go all the way with Thales —
Neptunism.
    Not so much shape-shifting as

losing shape altogether.
Spilling out into primordial albumen.
Liquidity.
Vahdat al-Vujud
as the Persian dervishes
put it.
Ab-i Hayyat the Water of Life.
Sitting on our picnic blanket
like Persians
in the jasper afternoon
sharing samovar & hookah
fresh herbs sheepsmilk cheese
pine nuts hempseeds & wine
or American equivalents
ham sandwiches beer & dope
we celebrate chaste nuptials
with imaginary nymphs of the
Esopus
born-again pagans
animist fundamentalists
naive realists
up to our hub-caps we ford the stream
follow dirt road to
return to the worldly world
all the way back to Calcutta-on-the-Hudson
Lower East Side suffocating night
the "red dust" as Han Shan calls it in

Cold Mountain Poems

Press Release

Vanishing Art no. II/5
"Swimming Hole Nymphaeum" (*riverpeople* Canto IV)
Monday June 6, 2011 (also Odilon Redon Day
& Festival of Chin Hsien, Taoist spirit of wine)

This small work was enacted to honor the nymphs & undines of the swimming holes of Esopus River, & especially Aegina, daughter of the rivergod Esopus of ancient Greece, who was raped by Zeus (in Canto III of *riverpeople*), my long poem-and-prose with history & hydrology of the Ulster Co. NY Esopus Kill.

Collaborators Raymond & Shiv drove down from Woodstock & we then proceeded to Stone Ridge in Marbletown, where we bought sandwiches & drinks for a Pic-nic. Then — to Tongore Road & the nice little rural park named after legendary Warranawarongkong Chief Tongore, on the Esopus in a former Indian cornfield, near "Fort Wyltmeet," the long-vanished Indian village. (See Canto VI for info on the Dutch/Esopus Indian Wars of the 1660s.)

A perfect (i.e. *normal*) June day, limpid & illuminated — park rather busy but not unpleasantly so — little league baseball game, old folks with dogs, a few kids swimming despite the NO sign, etc. We got there about 5 pm as afternoon was sliding slowly toward evening. We ate our sandwiches. We lit a few frankincense sticks. I took the little iron mermaid out of her shopping bag and began to fill her hollow body with appropriate symbolic jewels — i.e.: blue topaz earrings set in silver, aquamarine pendant with gilt clasp, freshwater pearl necklace & bracelet with cats-eyes & gilt clasps; and Shiv donated a green peridot, a moonstone, pieces of jade, turquoise & malachite, with a few cowrie shells & spiral shells from India, & a pinch of sage. (Total cost, with statue, about $125.) Into the bottom of the statuette I placed a folded color print of the *vèvè* of *La Siren* the Voudou goddess of water, inscribed to her on the back with a crescent moon & a prayer to her to protect the River. Then I sealed all with melted wax of a blue candle.

After a short informal "puja" to the now-empowered statue, we left Tongore Park & drove a couple of miles to the "swimming hole at an undisclosed location" eulogized in Canto IV, on the Esopus — a sort of beaver lake with downstream rapids, quiet & deserted, surrounded by shady trees (at the bottom of someone's farm), busy with wild ducks, redwing blackbirds & other species, all having a good old time.

We submerged the statue in a well-hidden (but still discoverable) place, lit some more incense, took pictures, & left quickly so as not to be *seen*.

Mermaid (Photo: Raymond Foye)

Thomas Cole, "Morning on the Hudson River"

Canto V/1
Pseudo-Sonnet for Dr Brink (1754–1843)*

The Enlightenment is a Good Ship Lollipop of which
we're the rattus norvegicus scuttling
ashore in rain-light sighing *sauve qui peut.*
Our guru knew that Dr Brink of Kingston
his enchanted forest now reduced to a few
tombstones in a suburban back yard backed
up to the exit ramp for Route 202
will supply us with graveyard gris-gris
quack-spagyric brews & slews of roots
& simples. Someone must've been thru
before us dropping breadcrumb clues
& influencing us with rural cunning
to pose as cryptic potentates &
nibelungize the Scenic Hudson View.

"Dr. Jacob Brink was a grandson of Dr. Jacob Brink, who was one of the early settlers of the town of Kingston, and who was familiarly known as the "old doctor." While not a member of what is known as the "regular school" of physicians, he was possessed of valuable healing qualities, which he exercised by manual application, and by which he is said to have effected many wonderful cures....

Dr. Jacob Brink (2d) was born on Sept. 29, 1808, and passed his earlier years on the paternal farm. His educational training was confined to that of the district school. Growing to years of maturity, he found himself possessed of the healing qualities of his grandfather, and these he exercised to a large extent during the remainder of his life, often rendering his services gratuitously, and successfully alleviating the physical ailments of large numbers of his fellow citizens....

Dr. Brink was a large, portly gentleman, having a full, open countenance, and possessed of a nature so genial and magnetic as to make him a man of great influence and popularity in his native town. Never a seeker after office, he was frequently placed by his fellow-townsmen in positions of trust and re-

* Originally published in *Black Fez Manifesto.*

sponsibility. For four-teen years he filled the office of assessor of the town of Kingston with acceptance, being first elected in 1858, and re-signing in the fifteenth year. He was supervisor of the town two years; was inspector of elec-tions a long time, and at the time of his death, on March 8, 1879, was president of the Pine Bush Rural Cemetary Association. He was connected with the Flatbush Reformed Church, where he filled the offices of both dea-con and elder."

Canto V/2
Dr Brink vs The Woodstock Witches

Send our regrets to Mrs Grimm
the witch who lived on top of Ohayo Mt
who gave that young Mr Bonesteel (7th son
                          of a 7th son)
                                    a hard time
stalking him & his fiancée one night
as a giant cat. He threw his boot at
Mrs Grimm's grin but the shoe passed thru
her spectral hologram. She specialized in the
                          hideous cackle:
terrorize the tourists & depress
                    real estate values.

Witchcraft should be taken seriously
in its negative black sense not just lovely
goddess worship but malignant
                    action-at-a-distance
such as television.
                    This is why in my house
I've got dirt from the grave of Old Dr Brink
seventh son of a seventh son & I'm
studying adapting his methodology — e.g. use meltwater
of Winter's last snowfall as ointment for eyes
red-sore with screenal bewitchment.

Superstitious by ideological conviction
sensual derangements fit
to induce amusing stupors vapors
& raptures in the unclean unclear
mentations of a self-induced dupe
or dope.

We saw the house where Dr Brink
        was born & dreamt up
his first anti-witch campaigns. It was
for sale. Gus Elmendorf's farm
where *Spook Hole* still disgorges the
occasional Indian or slave femur is
also for sale. The last old Mrs Brink
retired to Texas several years ago
to be near her daughter. She
was the one with the stories.
Everywhere
autos are blasting unfeelingly past
disturbing & dissipating the aether
leaving the sites of our researches
                sterile & dim.

In the 18th century darkness still
retained its reign & spawned healthy
        dread
of woods & crossroads & the
insinuating sniggers of unseen rills of
                unsleeping streams
but now
        night has changed & the entire Northeast
appears in satellite photos as the skin
of a radioactive leper. Dr Brink himself
might shrink in horror from this
vacuous glare like a scorned Lugosi.

The cure for light pollution must be
endarkenment.
                Power failure.
                        Reversion
to other powers still dormant in these
unnoticed hills.
                Note:
                        find
Dr. B's staff whip & bottle.
                Blessed by stars.
In black cloak & widebrim hat
striding down midnight lilac roads.

Channeling Dr Brink on crystal radio
stand where he stood. Replay his cases
                like chess problems

heavily charged tango's with
                    Hecate in overgrown graveyards
tangled with briar rose & blackberry.
                              He criss-cross'd
the starry vault of wisdom, a human balloon
looming above highways & parking lots that
pinch'd off
          the landscape's junky veins.
                              Recovering
from death's amnesia.
                    Planning
another reincarnation in Kingston
                    — another déja-vu-du.

Only certain families like the Bonesteels can act as messengers to fetch the Doctor
in emergencies — anyone else is like to meet w/ unexplained delays or accidents or get
lost along the way & arrive too late.
                    This is perhaps
the function of the text.
Benighted. Wandering
in circles. A whited sepulchre
w/ illegible hieroglyphs half
effaced. A séance that flops
due to the presence of skeptics.

Spook hole witches from the whole dark region
held walpurgisnacht sabbat in Hurley &
                              headless ghosts
loomed up at benighted backward riders.
Down a dirt lane this time we find
a bog where dead trees & poisonous weeds
guarantee a future devoted to nameless gloom.
                              Spook hole
resists the allure of improvement, a
sullen mere or tarn in the style
of some Punk Post-Industrial Poe. Leaden rays
occlude the cloudless day with an
oppressive haze. Nothing will thrive here
we'll never drop acid here on Halloween.
A make-shift descent to Avernus.
A slipshod bloodless sacrifice.

Indian graveyard slave graveyard
(no stones — they died like animals — or monks)
then it sinks deeper & deeper

                layers rub together
                        membranes wear thin
till seepage between dimensions begins.
Cows From Hell:

Pausanias gives it one star — "worth a detour.
A few ashen saddhus are squatting naked
                      passing around a smokestack
beneath druidic oaks. A Shrine to the Nagas.
Lepers. Irishmen beating each other w/
                      blackthorn clubs
in drunken glee. Penitenti. Patrick's
                Purgatorio."
But no. Just a trash dump. Just a
concrete pylon surrounded by vaguely
malignant weeds. Lenin plus electricity.
The vapid day. The susurrus of post-
                Fordist production.
Technology eventually becomes in itself
a form of mournfulness — an icon of
precisely what it has replaced suppressed
entombed beneath layers of smothered black
                velvet & mothballs:
premature burial — gasping for breath
a landscape can be re-shaped along
nodes of forgetfulness. Fear of death
is our last shared culture —

              terminal resentment.
No — it's machines they're haunted now
nature bereft of soul. Every lap-top
is a spookhole every cellphone a
                        radio from Hades
Rationalism the most widespread form of
                          the irrational
Place itself erased in all its non-Euclidean
                      geometries
its algorithm of numb greed &
                 hysterical puritanism.

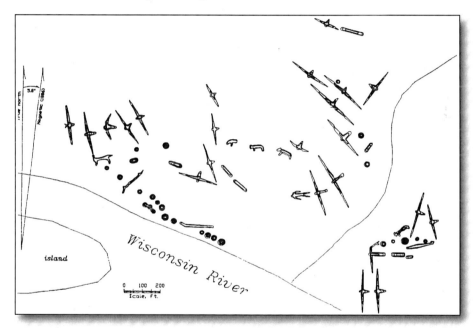

On the grounds of Mendoza State Insane Asylum in Madison Wisconsin a major
complex of Effigy Mounds incl. several giant Thunderbirds has been preserved, rumor
says they appear in healing dreams to some of the patients, each Effigy acts as focal
lens for different animate power
        — animating power
                — anima Monday
— Easter anyday — pantheist monism —
you risk insanity in order to bring back
healing words from the Ninth Sky
nobody wants them because they're not for sale
they're secret because worthless like the gospel
of the Christ Who Failed — who never
harrowed Hell — or redeemed Satan —
or any of his other alleged stunts.
His avatars along the Esopus include

riverpeople

Big Indian
Oscar Wilde
John Papunhank
Becky de Milt
Dr Brink
Esopus & Aegina
                          to name just seven
this book will have to be their spookhole
or hearing-trumpet for the bat-like gibbering
                                    of shades
                                                because
the place itself has been erased.

Thomas Cole, "Lake With Dead Trees, Catskills"

Canto V/3
Mink Hollow

Between the hamlets of Willow and Shady
Up the Beaverkill into Mink Hollow.
                                        Dark tarn.
These lilacs came originally from the Ottomans
                                along with tulips
as gifts to Rudolf II in Prague
in the days of the Golem & Dr Dee —
                        alchemical Rosicrucian Prague
always a haunt of witches. Today
we dig the truffles of Becky de Milt tall & thin
w/ coalblack hair & eyes & skin white
as snow — had a club foot — wore three
stockings on it — moonlit nights was seen riding
wild over mountain on her big black
stallion — Enemy Number One of
                        DR BRINK.

Right in the middle of Map 9
square P/36 where Mink Hollow Rd Crosses the kill
over a lone-lane bridge Becky's hut
                        stood just south of the stream
so she wouldn't have to cross running water
unnecessarily on her way into town —
                        always unpleasant for witches.

Becky hexed a local girl
to think she was a horse — "she
reared & snorted & stamped thru the night
in the morning there was the print
of a bit in her mouth" — Dr Brink
used a shawl stuck with pins
& his anti-witch riding whip &
saved the victim's sanity.

Dr Brink's direct ancestor Ernst
the antiquarian ambassador to
Constantinople in 1614 the very year
the first Rosicrucian manifesto appeared
might very well have introduced
                    lilacs to Holland
& perhaps his descendent Lambert Huybertson
brought lilacs to New Holland in 1659
on the ship *Beloove,* or Faith —
greatgrandfather of Dr Brink
                    & these lilacs
will add their Ottoman
amethyst pendulous clusters to our
Mink Hollow Cult
            of Doctor Brink

Canto V/4
Dr Brink, Fragments, Golden Crow

The reader is strongly urged to acquire Alf Evers's two masterworks *Woodstock* and *Catskills* — I met him in his 90s living in Shady, Ed Sanders introduced us, Alf was the Dean of Local Historians, not always *correct*, but great — if you follow up his bibliographic ref's & footnotes you'll soon know everything I know about Jacobus Brink & his family — *except* the location of his grave — which I will not give here — and the mystery of his Coat-of-Arms, which I shall (for the first time) expound herein — plus I've added some unpublished accounts (a typescript from Senate House Museum Archives in Kingston, & a few old newspaper clippings) concerning "Woodstock"-style witchcraft, which I (following Evers) believe to be quite a different phenomenon than New England witchcraft. Our variety here is more Algonkian & Dutch, more "folkloric" and less "Satanic" than the Salem variety — here it never led to any witch burnings as far as I know. Dr B's reputation was that he never killed a witch, altho he may well have given a heart attack to one or two of them in magical battles.

Historians might have noticed that Dr B was no illiterate peasant like the witches he battled or farmers he cured, but a book-reading professional of the landed gentry, with minor aristocracy amongst his forebears. But no one has so far noticed the very strong evidence that he belonged to a specific European tradition, Paracelsan & Rosicrucian, which at one time was also the predominant school of Natural Philosophy & Medicine in the New World as well.

Legend says that the "talent" for occult healing passed down in the family from our Dr B to his descendents. In folklore the Doctor's grandson, also named Jacob Brink, is often confused or conflated w/ his grandfather, so that the "Old Doctor" seemed to live from the mid 18th century to the end of the 19th (and even later) — like a Rosicrucian demi-immortal.

The "last" Brink with the talent never used it & died in 1936, or so they say. Family genealogy, however dull a pursuit, is the key to the Brink mystery (as to so many mysteries of history & para-history). The Gift did not originate with Old Jacob at his baptism in 1754; he himself inherited it as a family initiation, an occult heirloom. The clue lies in Heraldry, the study of the hieroglyphic emblems of kinship.

❖ ❖ ❖ ❖ ❖

Jacob Brink was baptized on Apr. 15 1754 at the Katsbaan Church, & died Dec. 30 1843. He married Christina Longyear & they had six children; she died three years after him. They're buried in Lake Katrine w/in walking distance of the old Brink house at the confluence of the Esopus & the Sawkill. (Becky de Milt's Beaverkill also flows into the Esopus, up near Mt Tremper, which explains why I've put both these characters, Becky & Brink, in a book about the Esopus River.)

The first Brink in the New World was Lambert Huybertse of Wageningen, on the right bank of the Rhine in Gelderland. A son, Cornelis, was born at sea during the voyage to New Amsterdam. In 1662 Lambert arrived at Esopus (i.e. the future Kingston) & acquired land in Hurley & Marbletown, built a house in Hurley that still stands, & founded a family. He witnessed several treaties w/ the Esopus Indians, & also languished with his wife & three children as their captives during the Esopus War, see next Canto. Lambert was Dr B's great-great-grandfather.

Young Jacob enlisted as a soldier during the Revolution in the First Regiment Ulster Co. Militia, & was detained in Manhattan during the British occupation. Jacob later owned three slaves. He served on the Woodstock Town Meeting in 1791 & was a pioneer settler in Woodstock; in 1804 he acted as Deacon at Shokan Reformed Church. Later he moved back down into the Valley. This fairly exhausts the documentary evidence for the Doctor's existence. Almost everything else is folklore.

❈ ❈ ❈ ❈ ❈

One thing that appears to distinguish Brink lore from that of lesser witch-doctors of the region (& they are legion) is the *inheritability* of the gift or talent for healing & magic. It runs in the family. "Seventh son of a seventh son" — or daughter. Secrets & learning are passed along with, what? magic genes? Does it skip generations? Is it transmitted from man to woman to man to woman, like certain Tantrik-Hindu initiations? Is it in the strict sense an initiation? or just blood?

Dr Brink II had several sons, but only one, Hiram, was said to have inherited the Gift. He supplied family lore to a folklorist, a Mrs. Gardner. The obituary already quoted calls Hiram "successful merchant" in Kingston, a deacon in the church, and a retiring sort of man who "avoided public trusts, & lived a quiet & unpretentioius life."

Dr Brink II's grandson Theodore (b. 1860) might also have inherited the Gift, since he inherited the magic Bottle (or "pottle") & showed it to Anita Smith, the Woodstock folklorist. "People whispered," wrote Evers, that power had descended to Theodore, postmaster & storekeeper at Lake Katrine; "but Theodore Brink made light of his gift" & died w/out a magical heir in 1936; "the days when witchcraft could dominate American minds was nearing an end," says Evers optimistically, forgetting the Satanic Abuse Panic as well as modern Wiccan-type witchcraft, which not only survives but thrives in the Hudson Valley. A witchcraft shop in my village was closed down a few years ago amidst rumors of animal sacrifice carried out in local graveyards.

Clearly the talent for white witchcraft passes *down* in the Brink family. But does it pass *up*? Does it have an origin in the far past & faraway Europe? If we knew what "it" was more precisely, we might be able to venture a guess as to where & when it originated.

❈ ❈ ❈ ❈ ❈

If I said that occult signs & intuition have convinced me that Dr Brink was a *Rosi-crucian,* my readers would have to shrug & smile, or snort, & give up. I have better (or anyway more scholarly) proofs. And I'll spare the reader a list of the "coincidences" & odd events that accompanied my Brink studies.

A footnote in Evers sent me to the series of articles on Brink Family genealogy in the journal *Olde Ulster,* written by its late editor, another Brink (Andrew) but sadly never completed. There I discovered among Jacob's ancestors in Holland one Ernst Brink, Burgomaster of Harderwyk in 1620. He "was a very learned man & cele-brated antiquarian…. From 1612 to '15 he was the secretary of the Dutch Embassy in Constantinople, & from 1618 to '48 librarian of the University of Harderwyk."

The years Ernst spent in Istanbul were the years the Rosicrucian manifestos first appeared in Germany & the Holy Roman Empire. Paracelsus had earlier been initiated in Constantinople, by his own account. Hermetic secrets & technology reached Ger-many & Italy from Constantinople, & aspiring Hermeticists made the trek to the Ot-toman Empire in search of knowledge once obtained in "the East" by Christian Rosy-Cross himself. The Rosicrucians pursued a policy of peace between Protestant states & the Turks, *against* the Pope.

Tulips & lilacs were first brought to Prague (& the magical court of Rudolf II) by an ambassador to the Sublime Porte. So tulips probably reached Holland via Rosicru-cian circles (they were cultivated especially by Sufis in Turkey); the actual agent, I like to think, could've been Ernst Brink. The dates would fit. If it wasn't him it was some-one very much like him. So… was Ernst the first Rosicrucian in the Brink clan?

Impossible to say. But somewhere in its history the family acquired an openly Her-metic *coat-of-arms.*

❊ ❊ ❊ ❊ ❊

The trick (i.e., the written description) for the blazon (picture) of Brink arms reads thus (w/ corrections of *Olde Ulster's* obvious errors of transcription):

> d'argent un boeuf de gueules
> corné d'or marchant sur une
> terrasse sinople. Bourlet et
> lambresquens d'argent et de
> gueules. Cimier: une corbeille
> d'or en sortant des flammes
> de feu

or, in plain English:

> on a silver background (the shield shows)
> a red bull hornèd gold, walking on a field
> of green. Flocked & mantled (i.e., the shield
> is draped with cloths) silver & red. The

> crest (i.e., helmet decoration): a crow
> of gold rising from flames of fire

Something like this:

The most dramatic part is the crest. The black crow (unclean uncanny trickster) commonly symbolizes the alchemical stage called *nigredo* or *putrifactio,* the lowest level of the Work but also the first step toward transmutation of that *materia prima* w/ which the alchemist must begin the Work. This *materia,* it is said, can be found on any dung hill — referring not just to dung itself but also to the subtle heat generated by such a heap, a process highly valued by the adepts. Putrefaction is a kind of fermentation, thus a fore-shadowing of the Work itself, the Elixir. Nature herself is in constant ferment, continual creation. In fact, *"low matter"* is already the Philosopher's Stone, at least to the true sage. As Goethe said, look no farther than the phenomenon itself, which is already the theory complete. For this reason the black crow is already secretly gold, like the Stone. Like the Phoenix, another symbol for the Stone or Elixir, our low crow re-births itself out of a nest of flames. In one sense this image refers to distillation & sublimation, two later stages of the operation, but already the crow "is" the final stage: as below, so above, for the realization of the Work, to paraphrase *The Emerald Tablet of Hermes Trismegistus.*

In the light of the crest we can interpret the shield alchemically also, altho its symbols are already glaringly Hermetic. The bull — one of humanity's most archaic religious symbols, basically symbolizing energy, also stands for the Stone (which is both red & gold) as living force; it grazes or strides however upon green grass, be-cause it is also a Spagyric Elixir based on plants, as well as a Stone based on metals (silver & gold).

Hermeticists generally agree that heraldry is one of the Hermetic arts, & some her-alds ("kings-of-arms") have admitted this to be true, esp. about late Germanic heraldry; Scottish arms are also supposed to be rich in Templar, Masonic & Rosicrucian motifs; &

so on. But rarely in heraldry does one come across so blatantly hermetic an image as the golden crow. For me it's proof enough of some connection between the Brink family & some Rosicrucian-type occultism. The evidence is circumstantial but very persuasive, given the family's later history. Dr Brink should be seen as part of the Rosicrucian tradition in the New World — which was far more widespread & important than any historian of American science has ever admitted (or even noticed).

❄ ❄ ❄ ❄ ❄

Viewed as folk Rosicrucianism, Dr B's "crude" charms take on new significance. The melt-water of the last snow-fall of winter reveals its medical use in its Paracelsan *Signature:* it embodies the very same occult principle as "the coolness of mine eyes" (as the Prophet Mohammad put it) because it *corresponds to* that blessed state; in a sense it "is" that state, just as the lion is the sun, or snakeweed the cure for snake bite. In spagryic medicine & alchemy these signs or links are considered actual (i.e., both material & spiritual) not merely allegorical. In the Paracelsan critique, so to speak, allegory is a null set. A descent, as W. Benjamin said, into pure melancholy.

Dr Brink's famous bottle of something made of seven herbs, colored black, which he dreamed in three nights, can now be seen as an Elixir of the Seven Planets. His knowledge of which plants belong to which planets could have come (directly or indirectly) from Culpepper's *Herbal,* Agrippa's *Three Books* or even from Marsilio Ficino's *Books of Life.* (Note: I also consulted the modern herbalist Cunningham, who generally seems to be a rectification of Culpepper.)

Dr B would've used locally available herbs as well as spices known to any Dutch cook. He would've looked to produce a general heal-all, a tonic against all negative planetary forces while emphasizing the positive. So, for instance, he could use nutmeg for the Sun (much praised by Ficino), which happens to be a psychoactive. For Moon, melissa (lemon balm), one of Paracelsus's favorites. For Mercury, mint, which Ficino never stops lauding. For Mars he could use wormwood, the psychoactive ingredient in absinthe. Jupiter could be clove (which *The Long Hidden Friend,* a contemporary book of Pennsylvania-German magic spells & herbs, is very fond of) but also sassafras, once thought to be a potent tonic. Saturn is a problem, since most Saturnian herbs are poisonous or highly psychotropic, such as hellebore or hemp. As we know however both were found abundantly in Colonial pharmacopeias. One solution would be ginseng, which is native to the Catskills (the Chinese buy a lot of it); according to Cunningham ginseng is magically the same as mandrake (because of the humanoid forms of the roots in both plants); and according to Ficino, Saturn rules mandrake. Finally for Venus, any local farm could supply the apple in the form of a distilled cider-brandy, white applejack, the very thing needed to make all the plants/planets agree in amorous harmony & flow together in a decoction or tincture of all the ingredients. If the resulting liquid were not black, it could be made so by coloring & sweetening it with molasses.

Old Doctor Brink's Planetary Elixir. And why not use poppy for the Moon? — then you'd've created a tasty form of laudanum, *the* most famous invention of Paracelsus, the true (probably Greco-Turkish) theriac or "cure-all." Dr B would've had no legal problems w/ such a potent patent spagyric; both cannabis & opium were quite legal. The pious Shakers of New Lebanon, over in Columbia County, made a great deal of money raising poppies for opium.

Note: Alf Evers, or possibly Hiram Brink, I think, made an error about "water taken from a running stream by scooping it up *against* the current." Theodore Brink told Anita Smith, the Woodstock folklorist, that "to be efficacious the salves had to be made from water running *with* the stream, not against it." The second technique is advocated by other magicians & seems correct symbolically.)

❊ ❊ ❊ ❊ ❊

Washington Irving actually met Dr Brink — & that meeting took place in an imaginal (but fairly real) landscape, one in which old-fashioned Dutch or German figures appear in a setting reminiscent of the Rhineland, with a few Indians lurking around in the shadows, a few Black slaves. The actual landscape however had come to include factories, mills, steamboats, canals & even railroads. Debunkers have often pointed out that the Hudson River School of landscape painting, & American Romantic artists & writers in general, tended to edit out or censor signs of industrialization & cultural homogenization from their compositions. Via Coleridge & Emerson the American artists & poets had absorbed the aesthetic theories of German thinkers like Schlegel & Goethe & their artist disciples such as Ph. O. Runge & Caspar David Friedrich. Many of the American painters were Swedenborgians or otherwise mystically inclined. Their goal was to express the hylozooism of the Romantic movement, the idea that nature is alive, the world is animate, in paintings that would serve as quasi-icons of a "religion of Nature." This "sacred theory of Earth" in turn represents the Romantic attempt to rectify & save the hermetic & Rosicrucian doctrines of Paracelsus & his fellow mages — the same tradition that gave birth to Johannes Kelpius of Pennsylvania, Justus Falkner his disciple in Upstate NY, Winthrop of Connecticut (a New England spagyric) & Dr Brink — that the Earth is a star (as Cusanus put it) & worthy of veneration. Nature is a *relation of identity*, as Novalis expressed it; science must be "poeticized." The Romantic reception of landscape is not a prettification or sentimentalization. Factories are not edited out simply because they're unpicturesque, but because they're sacriligious, like a Nike teeshirt on a Byzantine Christ.

The "gothic" aspect of this ideology or aesthetic theory can be seen, for instance, in the earlier work of Thomas Cole, his great allegorical landscapes, which are actually complex Emblems. Just as specific hermetic/alchemical vocabulary is edited out or rather hidden beneath the Romantic text, so the emblems disappear from Cole's later work, leaving only light itself as symbol of itself: the Illuminatus becomes a Luminist; nature itself is a perfectly adequate vehicle of contemplation when depicted from & as an interior state. Painter invited viewer to share experience of oneness with subject. Realism as Naturalism was never the goal; rather, the expression of the *real as ideal*. Real light is already the divine aura or aurora around every creation. This holds true from the earliest Hudson River School painters like Cole & Church to the latest, Blakelock for instance, a practising Swedenborgian, or Pinkham Ryder, who re-introduces Cole-like allegorical & emblematic gothicisms into his visionary land- and waterscapes.

Irving's eye emanated a "bourgeois gaze" that appropriated low & subaltern culture to its own self-consciousness. Fennimore Cooper, with his pseudo-aristocratic disdain for the actual poor (such as Anti-Renters or "vanishing" Indians, or "tri-racial isolate communities" like the Ishmaels) exhibits this colonial mentality in its most unpleasant manner. But Irving's motives were never so base: he showed his love for the old Dutch culture by poking gentle fun at it even as he gave it a halo of legendry (this was his "Romantic irony").

Not every "gaze" is evil; some gazes save what might otherwise be lost, & some elevate what they perceive thru a subtle alchemical sublimization. And, after all, Dr Brink was no noble savage innocent of his own being, exploited by consumers of an image divorced from actuality. He romanticized himself. He created his folk-rosicrucian persona. He cultivated charisma. He exaggerated himself in order to have healing power, both psychological & magical. He too was an artist.

Thomas Cole, "Home in the Woods"

Canto V/5
Mosaic of Quotations on "Woodstock" Witchcraft

The Witch-Doctor

Talking winter evenings with older residents of the valley has brought forth many tales of the souls claimed by the Mountain spirits. I have often told the stories of the old woman on Overlook who changed herself into a deer to leap around the cemetery and could only be hurt by a silver bullet, or the witch living near Indian Head Mountain who bewitched the little pigs, and of the old woman of Mink Hollow with one mishapen foot who could cast a spell by saying "Pocks-E-Rollins." This woman was like an ordinary neighbor most of the time, and she married and brought up a large family. Trouble arose only when she was crossed, and then with pride in her prowess she would evoke the help of the Devil and be enabled to do her will by bewitching the wheels to roll off a passing cart or to fly miles through the night to cast a spell upon a distant farm or to set a white cock to crowing at unseasonable hours to scare the wits from all who heard. Ordinary folks could only get the best of her by cutting a Witchhazel branch which was used frequently to "switch the Witches out of her skirt tails." Fortunately there were Witch-Doctors who could be called upon. From the great-grandson of one of the best-known Witch-Doctors I learned of his horseshoe cure and his laying on of hands which was usually accompanied by a medicinal pill that may also have assisted in the cure. This Witch-Doctor had a thriving practice from which he made a living until the law was passed preventing him from accepting fees for his services, however he still travelled through the country-side in his buggy bringing succor to bedeviled souls who in their gratitude would give him many gifts.

— Anita Smith

Hurley Witches. From Notes Given by Charles Dumond.

The whole country was full of witches; Jacob Bonesteel of West Hurley as a seventh son, had the power of fetching the witch doctor who lived in Saugerties. At one time, he went after the doctor and met with all sorts of difficulties before he could reach him, thrown in his way by the witches; he got mixed up with fences; was caught in trees and when he finally reached the doctor's, the foam could be scraped from his horse with a stick; the reason of this trouble by the witches was that the witches did not want him to see the doctor who alone could spoil the charms they put on people and so they

115

threw in the rider's way all these obstacles: when the man arrived at the doctor's, he came out, saw the trouble, wrote a few lines on a bit of paper, waved his hands, and Jacob went home without any difficulty at all....

An old witch lived in Beaverkill near West Hurley and after a while, she "dried up and blowed away."

A cardinal point to remember was, when sending for a witch doctor, not to allow any one to get in the room, otherwise a witch could enter and prevent the aid of the doctor.... A little girl was bewitched and Dr. Brink was sent for; while waiting for him, an old witch managed to slip into the room where the child lay; passing her hands over the child, the witch said "auntie has come to see you"; she then went out. When the doctor arrived, he saw that the witch had gained access to the child and told the parents it was too late; he could do no good. The witch had been in the room and thus prevented his doing any cure. He said though that he would punish the witch and taking a little shirt that belonged to the child, he cut it several times with a switch, saying the witch would have as many strokes on her back as he had given the child's shirt.

The witch doctor, Dr. Brink of Saugerties, had the power of killing a witch but never exercised it; he would punish her as he did in the above case but never kill them....

This was a great country; the animals had regular runs. When men went out hunting deer, the witches would often put a spell on the guns so that no one could hit a deer; but, load up with a bit of silver and the marksman was sure to hit.

An uncle of Dumond's was out hunting when he ran across a big deer; he tried a shot at the deer's side but the animal turned showing the other side to the hunter; he then suspected the trouble, put a bit of silver in his gun, fired but only lamed the deer; immediately a person in the neighborhood went lame.

His sister had a big fever sore on her leg; Dr. Brink was called; acting then in his capacity of a finger doctor, he rubbed the spot with his fingers using at the same time an incantation and caused the sore to disappear.

Hurley Spooks

The spook hole is the gully running from Hurley Avenue, near the Ulster line at Gus Elmendorf's, on the west side of the road. It has always born that name; Cornelius Hotaling was riding home one night from Kingston on horseback; on reaching this hole, his horse absolutely refused to budge an inch; no amount of whipping had any effect; finally, Cornelius got off his horse and looking through the darkness he spied a man standing by the road, against the fence, headless; some say the man carried his head under his arm; Cornelius mounted his horse, when he saw the reason of the horse's fright, took another direction and arrived home all right.

Witches and spooks were in the habit of gathering at the bottom of this hole or gully, hence the name.

— Dumond

Mombaccus Witches

D.F. — — — 3 Aug. 1900
An Interesting Letter from a Kerhonkson Man
Statement of Jan Van Doll Corroborated
Old Superstitions Not Yet Dead

Several weeks ago *The Freeman* published a communication from Jan Van Doll, in which that venerable gentleman spoke of the witches in the town of Rochester and how the people believed in them. The facts stated by Van Doll were not believed by a number of people, who could not imagine how any one, in Ulster county at least, could ever cling to the old belief in witches. The following self-explanatory letter in this week's *Ellenville Journal*, however, proves that Van Doll was correct, and it is of more than passing interest because it tells of people who are well known among the older residents of this city and county. The letter is from S. Wilkinson of Kerhonkson to Editor Taylor of the *Ellenville Journal*:

Kerhonkson, June 30, 1900

My Dear Taylor: Did you read Van Doll's story of the Mombaccus witches in *The Freeman* a day or two ago? These tales of a bewitched churn, of cows holding up their milk, etc., were currently told and believed in when I came here, fifty-seven years ago; and in fact, there are quite a plenty here who take stock in such stories yet.

The witch that Van Doll's aunt burned out of the churn with a heated horseshoe, and which was seen and heard to go screaming from the potato field, did not disturb the butter making or the cows of Van Doll's aunt any more. Indeed she was not seen out of her house again for a long time. A few years later she died; and in the process of preparation for her burial, the brand of the horseshoe was found upon her body.

That was the way the buttermilk witch story was told to me in the long ago by an old Dutch dame, who spiced the revelation with language that might seem indecorous in print.

Were my friend Van Doll to visit the scenes of his youth he would learn that the old superstitions are not yet dead — if the witches are. And I believe that he would find a few of the witches "doing business at the old stand."

The good people of Mombaccus and Rochester still consult the moon, when they plant their beans and cabbage. And wisely, too, for cabbage, if not planted by the moon (not in it) will head in the ground; and beans will not climb poles, except they be set out in the climbing of the moon.

Van Doll says his aunt's bees were bewitched. I never heard of that; but I know that they were wont to go and tell the bees of every death in the family, or it was said the bees would swarm and go away. My brother-in-law was a bee keeper, and as I know, he used to go around amongst his bees and tell of all the misfortunes in the family. There are people who wouldn't for their lives sit at table in a company of thirteen persons; nor would they dare to begin any important piece of work on Friday.

Your truly,
S. Wilkinson

Daily Freeman
August 3, 1900
(Kingston, NY)

Witch in Black

D.F.   5 Feb. 1901
At Mettacahonts
Chased by a Constable She Dissolves Into a Vapor
The Story of One Night's Exciting Events
This Woman in Black Must Be a Witch

People in the town of Rochester are very much excited over what seems to be a reappearance of the old-time witches, such as were written about a few months ago by Jan Van Doll and Mr. Wilkinson. The mysterious performances of a tall woman attired in black, and wearing a black veil, are the causes of the excitement. At first it was thought that she was a government detective bent on some important mission, as detectives are known to always disguise and conduct themselves in a manner to attract as much attention as possible, but later developments proved beyond a doubt that the woman is possessed of supernatural powers, and the general impression now is that she is a witch of the true Mombaccus breed.

The veiled woman first appeared in a country store in Rochester one evening. She carried a pint bottle, and demanded that it be filled with laudanum. None of those in the store knew her, and there was great curiosity felt and expressed. Later she appeared again on the same errand. It was then supposed that she was a detective seeking evi-

dence that laudanum was sold without the proper label. Later it was reported that a mysterious woman in black had stopped a man on the road from Kripplebush to Lysonville one dark night, and also that the bandits who robbed a Rosendale constable one night were women dressed in black and wearing black veils.

As the matter was further discussed around the stoves in the country stores and the returns from the back districts came in, it was found that many had seen the woman. At Millhook, Whitfield, Mettacahonts, Accord, Mombaccus, Kyserike, Alligerville, Tabasco and other places she had been seen by terror stricken men, women and children.

Finally the climax came one night at Mettacahonts, when even scoffers had to admit that the woman in black really existed, for she appeared to a score or more of people assembled in a country store. Those who saw her say she was as big as two ordinary women, was well dressed in black, and wore a black veil over her face. They did not wait to interview her, but all hastened out into the fresh air. Constable Charles Rider, who has a reputation for fearing neither man nor demon, was summoned, he having frequently said that if he got a chance he would capture the woman. Headed by the constable, the crowd started after the woman, who ran with superhuman speed along the road. At times it appeared as though her feet did not touch the ground. The crowd was gradually distanced, but the constable, whose past experience in chasing criminals gave him an advantage, kept up the pursuit, and seemed to gain. Slowly he overhauled the fugitive. The rest of the pursuers were far behind, around a turn in the road, when the constable came within reach of the woman. He stretched out his hand to grasp her fleeing form when she vanished into vapor. Where she had been there was nothing.

Ralph Albert Blakelock, "Moonlight, Catskills"

Canto V/6
On The Brink

                    ultimately you can't
tell witch doctors too clearly from witches
the dialectic (if there is one) floats & dissolves
                              in mist
coalescing from time to time in
                         tableaux vivants
of terror & exaltation, each Effigy
                         or rebus
based not on flat one-to-one allegories
but Signatures & Correspondences.
                         Nothing
can be counted or accounted for
                    except sudden incursions of
unpredictable inexplicable non-verifiable
                         not-for-profit
'pataphysically palpable but immeasurable
powers of the spirits
secret class war carried on clandestinely
since the Neolithic — a never-ending
                         rearguard action
steady retreat toward & into the West
                         Hell or Connaught
                         Oklahoma or Bust
                         Indian Territory
suddenly Dr Brink & the Witches
in their dialectical dance belong to
                         one world
                              fading
soon to be declared   dustbin of volkishness
                         defunct & meaningless
witch & witchdoctor equally doomed to
cardboard cut-out Halloween masks
all spooks erased by glare of electricity
satanic parody of technoconsumerist

5th-rate trance state
the subconscious like an old mole refuses
                              to evolve
locked in double helix with the MechanASM
all machinery is juju to this reptile brain

Dr Brink & Ms. de Milt of Mink Hollow
both suddenly Christs
                    failed messiahs
icons in the Church of Holy Endarkenment
our lord'n'lady of the last possible Outside
rebels against the Future.

Dutch African Algonkian Anglican
                              Santeria
thick as salmagundi
                    rhizomatic as mold
negative capability
                    mass hallucinations
                        (i.e., perfect art)
When Dr. B met Washington Irving in Hurley
this revolutionary recalcitrance was both
flattened & universalized into an
ideology concealed w/in the faux-antiquarian text
& flowed together in one last magical uprising —
the Anti-Rent War of 1845 — first
                of the Romantic Revolts
                              Farmer Browns
browned off fed up with centuries of feudalism
crossdress themselves up as Indian women

burn barns — tar-&-feather a few
                                        bailiffs
ride by night like Herne the Hunter's
                                        Infernal Rout
torchlight chants & false faces — war
of Image Magic power of the powerless
Down With Rent echoes Indian critique of land
                                        as property
Calico Indian pow-wows & dances
kinte-kaying devil worship at the Danskammer
                Walpurgisnights of
                        Woodstock witches

deliberately squinting to block out
everything since 1979, 1911, 1845... directed gaze
of antiquarian obsessive fetishism
beams on this now-officially-disenchanted
                                        scapescape
looking only to be spooked, will be spooked
haunted by visual sur- and infra-
                        somatic
evidence of views out of Rodolphe Bresdin
Odilon Redon
                nature ensouled &
saturated with unnatural light.
All the acid I took in Millbrook
at Leary's LalaLand in the Sixties
imprinted me w/ the Occult Hudson Valley meme
— Jesus is a mushroom — and ever afterwards
little flowers in crannies are whispering
hoodoo messages —
                        icy kills &
                                old snow
writing frosty alphabets on retinas
semi-permanent flashback vision
                                mystic oneness of
                                        animate earth
                                                etc.
because when you've got the Rosicrucian Key
to the Big Mysteries right there in yr
                                        left hand
as you write w/ right you can almost
drift
back or sideways to certain versions
with a crank-powered victrola

shellac discs
ear-shaped horn amplifier
emerald needles
to be a people that must sing
to get anything clear
at all
would be worth the danger of a little
witchcraft
covens even now plotting the downfall
of Civilization & its replacement by
the Neo-Neolithic — return to the
Dark Ages —
when everybody played an instrument
everyone knew the Constellations
anybody
could knapp flint & practice
arts of venery
leave no trace on the land
pagan deities
filled us with lusts
— what to do?
So what?
set off a few bombs
re-enchantment bombs
bomb ourselves back to the Stone Age
w/ Buster Keaton's black anti-Kop bomb
flying like a crane between Dr Brink & the Witches
amidst Persian-Chinese clouds expressing
the baroque uncertainty principle
for those who treasure
divine vagueness
clumsy
unfinished
& yet
most exquisite

Press Release
Vanishing Art #8 (*riverpeople*, Canto V)
"Dr Brink and the Woodstock Witches"
Oct. 31, 2010 (Samhain/Halloween)

Dr Jacob Brink practised as a "witch doctor" and healer in the Kingston/Woodstock area. He met Washington Irving. And he passed into legend and folklore (how many of us will be able to make this boast?)

He came from a Dutch family of "folk rosicrucians," and his descendants also practised the healing art. His grandson, also named Jacob Brink, is often conflated in folktales with his grandfather, the original model, so the character "Dr Brink" appears to live on for about 150 years, like some legendary alchemist. A number of other relatives also inherited the mantle, including a "white witch" of Schoharie Co., and the "last" died in the 1930s.

On page 100 you see the house where the first Dr Brink was born, and his real grave (right), both very near the confluence of the Sawkill and the Esopus River, in Lake Katrine. (Finding this grave involved a fair bit of research.)

Dr. Brink's story has become Canto V of my long "epic," *riverpeople,* all about the Esopus River, its numinous history and hydrography. You can read all about Dr Brink in *Wilderness to Woodstock* by the late dean of local historians Alf Evers, whom I was honored to meet (thanks to Ed Sanders) a few years before he died. (We talked mostly about the Jukes.) I'm unable to add anything much to Alf's account of Brink, except for my discovery of alchemical symbolism in the Brink family coat-of-arms, suggesting that the family "gift" was indeed ancient.

Evers also wrote about the Witches of Woodstock — a fairly huge topic. Catskill witchcraft differed from the New England variety by being more Indian-influenced, more volkish and less "satanic." No witches were ever executed in New York State —

altho Dr Brink's counter-magic (his "witch-whip") may have resulted in one or two fatalities (or not — the legends differ on this). Moreover, like Pennsylvania-"Dutch" hex doctors, our local magi were scarcely in good odor with church authorities, who suspected that they would perform rituals of dubious morality if paid to do so; i.e., that "witch doctors" were simply another category of "witch."

One of Dr Brink's most famous antagonists, Becky de Milt of Woodstock, is described as beautiful, with dark hair and eyes, but with one withered leg. She dressed all in black and rode an all-black stallion. She lived on Mink Hollow Road, out along the Beaverkill, which flows into the Esopus near Mt. Tremper. (Thus two streams, Brink's Sawkill and Becky's Beaverkill, both originate in Woodstock and both join the Esopus — this being the hydrotopic aspect of our story.)

Evers recounts several run-ins between Dr Brink and Becky de Milt, which I've lifted for my *riverpeople* text (along with my own notes on early Rosicrucianism and "pagan" history of the Hudson Valley).

I've also noted that areas of our region rich in witch-lore happen largely to coincide with areas where Anti-Rent War actions flared up around 1845, which leads me to consider local witchcraft as a kind of sub-political resistance to Church/State/landlord oppression. (In this I follow the theories of Margaret Murray and Carlo Ginzburg.)

My "art action" for Halloween was devoted to promoting both a *revival* of and a *reconciliation* between Becky and Brink — between the witches and the witch-doctors — since both kinds of magic stand strategically opposed to the vulgar materialism and boredom and landscape-disenchantment of too-Late modernity; both are equally necessary for the kind of *ecological alchemy* proposed by my Vanishing Art Series. For me the battle of Doctor Brink *vs* Becky becomes a kind of dance or ceremony in which dark and light are "married" according to Rosicrucian/Tantrik principles, on a level where discord becomes strange harmony.

In order to symbolize and realize this intention I carried out the following preliminary steps on October 3 (with Raymond, Chuck, Shiv and Rachel):

a. A pilgrimage to Dr Brink's grave with flower offering. Collected and saved a few flower petals and some graveyard dirt ("gris-gris.") We then paid a visit to the Brink House, where we met the present owner, who nicely invited us to explore and photograph all we liked, he said he hadn't been bothered by ghosts since he'd built a little house for them in a hollow tree on his lawn. [I guess he was joking…]

b. A pilgrimage with flowers to the site of Becky de Milt's long-vanished cabin on the Beaverkill (just before the bridge). Saved a few petals and also collected a bottle (Blue) of water from the stream, according to the true instructions of Dr Brink (*with* the current not *against* it). By the streamside we found a beautiful old rusty shovel, like something by Joseph Beuys, propped up and just waiting for us to pick it up and use it in this work.

c. Made up a medicine bag (called *paquette Kongo* in Voudoun) containing the gris-gris and the petals from both sites along with St-John-the-Conqueroo and some SHIV Brand Holy Ganges River Ashes, a crystal *vajra* (actually a Long Island Indian arrowhead), a piece of magnetite and some iron filings, a few grains of amber — to produce a subterranean "organic electromagnetism" that will broadcast itself on the Akashic level.

Sunday Oct. 3 was brisk and sunny, the first real October day. The streams were full and rushing — leaves just starting to change. All my actions this year (so far) have been blessed with perfect weather. Perhaps all magic is (also) weather magic?

On Halloween I will (Inshallah) finish this piece, "Dr. Brink vs the Woodstock Witches," in Woodstock, in Shiv Mirabito's back yard, around sundown. Previously I had purchased the skeleton of a toad from Carolina Scientific Supplies (for about $200) — it came mounted under a perspec box. I will open the box, fill it with honey, then seal it shut again (with epoxy and beeswax), with the skeleton still visible thru the golden fluid.

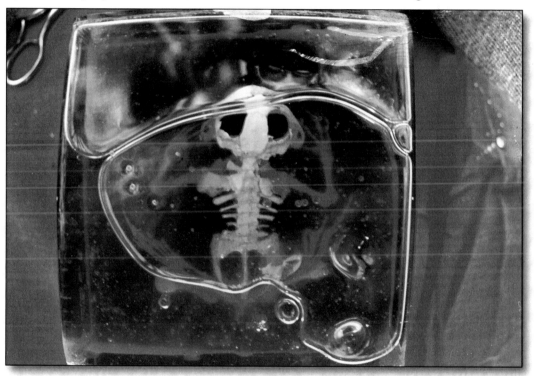

Toad Skeleton in a Vitrine of Honey
(Photograph by Neil J. Colligan)

I will then dig a hole in the back yard of Shiv Mirabito, my art & poetry comrade, near his famous saddhu's fire pit and outdoor altar, where so many revels and poetry *mushairas* have taken place; I will use the Becky de Milt Memorial Shovel to dig the hole; then I'll lower the toad and the paquette Kongo into the hole and bury them; and I'll pour the witch-water over the loose earth, using a Hindu water-ladle and ritual spoon (gift of Shiv).

This Halloween action will bring to a close the first druidical year of my Vanishing Art works; number one was "Mombaccus," carried out on Halloween '09 (Samhain is the Celtic New Year's Day). Next year (Spirits willing) I hope to finish the Esopus River series, and produce a major work devoted to Iuppiter & the Winds & Aires, at the spectacular Plattclove Gallery high atop the "Wall of Manitou" (the road up the Clove is so vertiginous and primitive it has to be closed all Winter).

This first year has been largely devoted to Earth and Water, next year (inshallah) more largely to Fire and Air. I also hope to do a big work in honor of the vanished local Natural Ice Trade. I hope to launch the *Seven Churches* project, an elaborate multiple work, for Non-Juring Anglicanism and the *re-paganization of monotheism*. [Note: one of the churchyards holds the grave of Mary Cragin, sometime resident of Rondout (Kingston), lover of John Humphrey Noyes, co-founder of Oneida Community, champion of Free Love, who drowned in a shipwreck in the Hudson River in 1851 (See Alf Evers' book on Kingston, a true radical heroine and martyr.)]

In memory of Janine Pommy-Vega, died Dec. 23 '10.

POST SCRIPTUM ON HALLOWEEN

Jim Fleming and Lewanne Jones drove me up to Woodstock. Lewanne shot a film of the day's action to send to a film festival in Barcelona. About 25 people showed up, incl. Andy Clausen & Janine Pommy-Vega, Carey Harrison, Donald Lev, the Quashas, the Potters, various friends of Shiv (James, Neil, etc), Kim Spurlock & his kids, plus the usual suspects Chuck & Raymond, and Nathan & Roberto. Weather was overcast & cool; Shiv's saddhu fire felt pleasant. I burnt masculine frankincense, Hekate blend & Seven African Powers. I explained the action in a ten-minute "sermonette." Andy & Kim helped dig the hole. A huge flock of turkey buzzards hovered overhead during the proceedings; a gate flew open without touch of hand or wind; and as we finished & were saying goodbye it began to *snow* very gently.

Canto VI
The Esopus Wars

            temporary as deer or bear or blue heron
their Prophets and Prophetesses preached
refusal of metal glass loomed cloth
guns alcohol everything post-neolithic
like Irish Fairies they hated metal
                  modernity, money
                        Christian morality
Civilization's tsunami.
                  Return to Nature's Way
            power against *Europe*.
                    I heard exactly the same stories
in Java in 1980 — magic invulnerability — magic weaponry —
politics of sorcery — messianic expectations — return to
ancestral custom
             against agriculture
             against the State
                  & its cannibal
                      high priests
never ceased from 4004 BC to the 6th millennium
                  foretold by Revelation
Stone Age reactionaries
               speechlessness
Masonic "words"
        gestures of distress
             occult handshakes
cacogenic traits
        atavistic sullen lazy
        immoral doomed by DNA
— Degenerate Traditionalism — how's that
for a bumper sticker
               failure is our last forest
                  no wonder
this passion for Vanishing Art
                missing people
        palpable even in their
             evanescence

Hermetic Universalism came to be rooted in the late Hellenistic doctrine or praxis called the *Interpretatio Romanorum* whereby an Egyptian or Mesopotamian deity could be *identified* with a Greek, Roman, Celtic, Norse, Syrian, Iranian or Indian deity. For example, Mesopotamian Nebu "IS" Egyptian Thoth — Greek Hermes — Roman Mercury — Celtic Lugh — Norse Odin — Hindu Budh — etc. Late Classical Paganism can thus be seen as a congeries of cults, sects, mysteries & practices (such as alchemy) which could be experienced both as multiplicity & as continuum, an infinity of differences smoothed out in space as a spectrum of identities — chaste chaotic coherencies. *Santeria* exhibits precisely this spirit of Hermetic Interpretation when it identifies Christian saints w/ African orishas on the basis of "Signatures." Chango the god of iron "is" St Barbara, who was martyred by iron implements. But there remains a *deep* identity as well — a defiance of mere gender.

If the religion of the Esopus Indians is "lost," it can be re-imagined via the *Interpretatio*, which is not limited to diffusionist history but also englobes structural universals. That is, humans qua humans share certain immutable archetypes based on the body & on its consciousness of the world of Nature. In what essential way do the Three Sisters of Corn Beans & Squash differ from Ceres Flora & Pomona? Leni-Lenape/ Munsee religion in any case is not dead. A movement to restore the ceremonies of the *Long House* certainly exists & even thrives, inshallah. Inasmuch as these rituals belong to certain families I have no interest in "appropriating" them. However I cannot imagine pretending not to be in-spirited to enthousiasmos by the traditions that once shaped the very landscape I now inhabit.

The vanquishing & disappearance of the Esopus Indians is a tragedy. But its tragic agony afflicts not only the victims but also the perpetrators of the Esopus Wars. The Dutch & English lost precisely by winning — they lost the *near presence* of hunting/gathering/gardening non-authoritarian tribal culture as a potential antidote to the poisons of Civilization w/ its "moralic acid" & materialist bathos. Loss upon loss then followed – above all, loss of any concept of sacred landscape, not to be rediscovered till the 19th-century Romantic movement, but now once again threatened by the penumbra of a terminal technopathocracy.

Hypothesis: Esopus society had long ago attained a collective consciousness based on shared consensual perception of animate Nature that made no clear distinction between material & spiritual. The great Irish Neo-Druid Freethinker & first English translator of Giordano Bruno, our hero John Toland coined the word pantheism to describe this worldview with its correlative mental state of waking dream or social mythopoiesis.

> Amateur local historians
> based on hearsay faulty memories
> legends hagiographies trunks of old letters
> manuscripts of lost forgotten cults
> your work appears in yellowed newspapers
> reduced to fragile microfiche or
> > fugitive pamphlets.
> Old public library history ladies (& the odd gent)

I revere you, parasitize you for poetry
                              through you
touch the past w/ imaginal mind probes
& psychometric trance states
                        — without you
it's all nothing but real estate
                        viewshed
empty spaces between A and B
but out of focus — devoid of
                        taste touch smell.

    ❀   ❀   ❀   ❀   ❀   ❀   ❀

I hate the fucking Esopus Wars
don't want to describe them.
                        Read
Ruttenber's *Indian Tribes of Hudson's River* (1872)
surprizingly pro-Indian & anti-racist for the period
squarely blames it all on the Dutch
                        shot an Indian woman
                              for stealing a peach
after all, not a native fruit but imported
by Europeans originally from Persia — *peche*
                              means the Persian fruit
thence to the New World — a biologic invader
péché — sin — the original Edenic fruit
St Augustine & the apples of Tunisia
that peach led step by karmic step
                  to the Esopus Wars
massacres burnings taking of captives
scalping torture — the human usual.
Gov. Stuyvesant, he of the ivory peg-leg
betrayed the first peace treaty by selling
several Indian hostages off to slavery
                        in Curaçao
                              the final straw.
Among the prisoners held by the Esopus, Evert Pile
had murdered several Indians
                        they determined
                              to slay him
but at last moment "chief's daughter" stepped forward
in accordance with old custom & adopted the captive
in forest's depth he became her husband
                        when all prisoners
were finally released she was unwilling to

part w/ him or he w/ her — they returned
to the wilderness to share their fortunes
                                        & freedom
— another White Indian
                        — converted to paleolithism
— lost to
            Civilization.

Naming names
                "liberté libre" as Rimbaud put it
requires leaven of
                    forgetfulness
taboos on names of the Dead & the
                        oppression of *what really happened)*
but also
            — how ego
descends from an Animal such as Wolf or Crow
in wavelike generations — heraldry
                        the first paleo-dialectic.
Wampum is neither money nor writing in "primitive" form
but a heraldic-style symbol-system designed to *prevent*
just such disasters from occuring —
                                    perfect gift of a
                                        Gift Economy
                            Fathoms of useless gems in
                            magic patterns of
                            affinity or condolence
                            — Long Island clams

Dutch anti-alchemists turned wampum into money, learned how to counterfeit
shellbeads with glass, used lunatics at the asylum to churn it out & corner the market.
Soon came the first American "bank crisis" — the crash. Originally wampum was a
magic Memory Palace (very like Giordano Bruno's) — not government archive
    nor damnable medium of exchange
    but vortex of images
                    creative forgetfulness
                        blessed illiteracy.
A people without books wld be a free people
— tribe as theater — the Forest sings us — etc.
where each rock & tree can speak —
                            all our relatives —
essentially the Hermetic Doctrine of Signatures
as above so below spirit & matter
                            modes of consciousness
essentially Novalis. Goethe. Thoreau.

It's turtles all the way down
                     as the old woman says

If I'd been Munsee in the 18th century
I'd've been ultra Paleolithic Traditionalist
Luddite (anti-metal) anarcho-primitivist
like the Delaware Prophet's gang
                                    but
as historian of religions I know
these nativist doomsday messianic ghostshirt-type
last-ditch revivals of lost Stone Age Edens
always fail
               even tho they are correct
                         & thus resemble
Xtianity itself — the messiah
               always executed
                 by the State
always fails to Return at any Second Coming or
No-Show Apocalypso
               — so —
                     why not skip
the apologetics & simply say Jesus died
like the Delaware & Munsee Prophets w/ their mystical
symbolic charts of deerskin delivered to
every village: — quit drinking firewater — stop
                         intertribal war —
worship old spirits — revive old customs —
seek visions — rise up in final armageddon
against the oppressor & embrace
the *Christ Who Failed*
     the wounded alchemical Jesus of
              Count von Zinzendorf or Blake
— yes — Druid Freemasonry — why not —
humans are made to be haunted
why not beautiful spirits rather than ugly —
beautiful & doomed to fail
                  Disappearance as Will to Power
Lord of all Game & Polar Axis Mundi
Celestial Bear — subject of the Mass —
                    slain & eaten
betrayed & worshipped
                    wildness over domestication
venery as venery —
              to love is to eat —
divine food chain of the *Rig Veda*.

White Crow lights the pipe
                              some boyscout fantasy
metaphorical wilderness
                         make-believe ballroom
                                        sad suburb
of New Jersey w/ its Indian place-names
choked in lacquer of tar & concrete
                              Leave Civilization Behind
become an Indian like so many 16–17th century runaways
or "captives" who refused to be ransomed
to the dismay of Cotton Mather
satanic as witches & all who
defy their own godgiven lowness & dare
rebel against God's annointed
                              sociocrats & Kops.
HARMONY as pictured by Green Hermeticism
                         & the Munsee Prophets.
Swedenborg Fourier Hiyawatha — smash
the rhizomatic panopticon of universal
                              surveillance
return to dark forest
                   reveries
reversion & endarkenment.
Escapism. Impossibilism.
Messianic significance of the
                         missing Munsee families
the Hekans and Nimhams etc.

                    Pipe is cold.
Nothing remains but
                   tainted nostalgia.
Museum orgies. A
                   crucified/resurrected
                   lost/found
                       nation.
A Consolation.

It seemed
I had to understand
lost words of the Delaware Prophet
Neolin: give up all metal & return
to Neolithic purity — & Munsee Prophetess
                              old lady *Beate*
who revealed the final form of Big House *xingwikaon*

134

using no nails glass or other Euro trash
or John Wilson part-Delaware prophet
of Big Moon Ceremony peyote religion
preached to the Absentee Delaware 1880s
                              & later in Oklahoma
                                  (Anadarko)*
can offer no solutions to the problem of technopathocracy other
than sabotage or passive resistance — which is at least A PLAN.
Even Escapism cld be a form of revolt
— Endarkenment — voluntary refusal of
Enlightenment Progress Efficiency —
embrace superstition & animism —
magic spells for a landscape
already bereft & reduced to
the empty spaces between home
                              shopping &
                          work.
                                  Speak
to an absentee hearer
                      — vanishing art —
these sacred places
                  are not listed
                                  — mostly
unmarked & largely forgotten —
                                  invisible
including the Indian. And
the art too is "gone" — it exists
only in the very moment it vanishes —
leaving behind itself
faint traces of its
passing — lingering
                  scent.

* Harry Smith, Lib. of Cong. *Peyote Rituals:* "Now this was recorded in some hotel in Anadarko,
  Oklahoma; or in some *other* hotel in Anadarko, Oklahoma…"

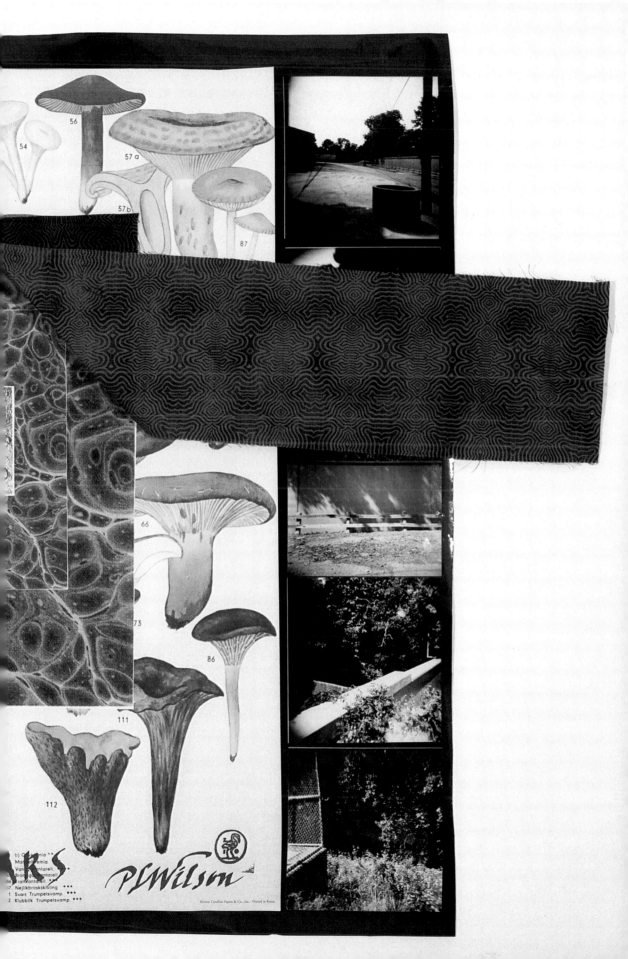

Press Release
"The Esopus Wars"
Vanishing Art #6
(Canto VI of *riverpeople*)
Tuesday, July 13, 2010

Legend says violence broke out between the Dutch and Indians when a Dutch farmer caught an Indian woman stealing a peach from his orchard — and shot her. "Peach" is originally and etymologically the *Per∫*ian fruit or *pêche* — a botanic "invader" of the New World — exotic even in Europe, and in China sacred — like the apple of *Genesis*. The event somehow seems "uncanny." Karmically, tit for tat, massacre by massacre, this theft and murder led to the Esopus Wars of 1659–1664.

Over the past year I've managed to identify and visit all the Esopus Indian settlement sites mentioned in Ruttenber's 1872 classic *Indian Tribes of Hudson's River* and Evan Pritchard's *Native New Yorkers*. I learned that each of these sites has the same "feng shui"

so to speak. A low flat ridge at a bend in some small canoe-navigable river adjacent to seasonal floodplains (planted with corn, beans, and squash, the "Three Sisters") is always found near mountains for winter hunting, marshes for gathering and trapping, water weirs for good fishing, etc. Up on the ridge a circular log palisade would protect five or six large communal wigwams and a communal Long House ("temple"). The Dutch called such palisaded villages "castles"; these included "Wyltwick" and "Wyltmeet" (*wylt:* "wild man") on the Esopus River itself; a settlement on the Roundout (at present-day Fort Ben) called Ankerop's Castle or Wawarsing; one on the Wallkill at New Paltz's museumized Huguenot Street; and one on the Shawangunk Kill.

All these castles were burned down during the Wars — but even now all the sites — (except one) — still preserve a shadow of the authentic Algonkian aesthetic landscape, which was sacred to its in-dwellers, and of course naturally beautiful.

When Henry Hudson "discovered" (dire word!) the Esopus Indians, they would have been recognized by anthropologists like M. Sahlins or P. Clastres as a non-authoritarian roughly egalitarian hunter/gatherer/gardening society, engaged in occasional ritual/primitive wars but generally peaceful, with a rich shamanic spiritual life amidst a setting of natural plenitude that left a great deal of "leisure" free for daytime naps, woodcarving, dancing and vision-questing. The more I studied them, their religion (fragments of which persist in later Munsee folklore) and their "organic anarchism" so to speak, the more I admired them.

One day I was doing something at the Kingston Plaza Mall, a hideously ugly block of useless commodity traps with incredibly vapid public muzak, an abandoned railway track, and a vast hell-realm parking lot, when I suddenly noticed that the Esopus River, which flows behind the Mall, is contained and virtually hidden behind a huge metal dyke. I realized then that I was standing in the Esopus Indian floodplain cornfield known as Athar-Hackton. I looked up and saw the flat ridge where Wyltwick Castle would've stood — now the site of the Senate House Museum. It all became clearer: Wyltwick was… uptown, "historical" Kingston. The Mall parking lot was… the actual battle site of the first Esopus War.

Aha.

Canto VI concerns the Esopus Wars. Each Canto serves as documentation for at least one Vanishing artwork or temporary landscape installation. Canto VI is the darkest and most depressing section, far more tragic than Canto III on the Ashokan Dam/Reservoir, which at least looks nice and provides some of us with clean water. The tragedy consists of the total/virtual disappearance of the Esopus Indians from our bioclime. Across the Hudson some Wappingers still reside, and I know of a few Munsee-descended locals (all poets, oddly) — but the Esopus are present here only as ghosts. Their nearest descendents live far away in Ontario. Their absence lies at the heart of the historical *disenchantment* of this landscape. And of all the psychic-poisoned spots along the river, the Kingston Mall and Dyke may be the most ugly, abject and haunted.

To commemorate the War at the Mall I decided to make another druidic "water deposit" or sacrifice of valuable things. I feel the spirits cannot be sloughed off with cardboard pentagrams and botanica candles (tho' these have their place). Real sacrifices must be made, which nowadays requires some outlay of *money* — which is, after all, an authentic Hermetic substance.

I collected the following objects for inclusion in a Crane Medicine bag:

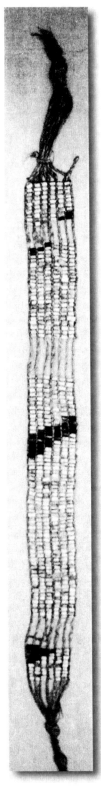

Tobacco for Native spirits. (Aleister Crowley says tobacco makes ideal incense for Mars god of War.)

15 wampum beads (10 white, 5 purple) modern but authentic

5 authentic arrowheads from Kentucky

5 authentic rock crystal arrowheads from a dig on Long Island (symbolic for me of lightningbolts, vajras)

5 replica arrowheads of black obsidian

a one-lb. block of catlinite (red pipestone from Minnesota)

5 Indian Head US pennies

5 Buffalo/Indian US nickels

Total cost of above, about $150

Plus: a bead of amber preserving several extinct insects (Costa Rican) from Carolina Scientific Supplies, $90

and two peachstones.

If this collection coheres as a kind of "spell" then its purpose would be:

a) an epitaphic offering to the forgotten and offended spirits of warriors, etc.

b) an attempt to spiritualize even this Ugly Space — so banal it's almost picturesque — in the minds of those who hear of my action;

c) an attempt at reconciliation — hope for the *return* of the Indians and the "re-wilding" of the Hudson Valley.

Almost the only remaining Esopus Indian artwork, a wampum belt created to mark the peace treaty betwen the Esopus and the English — (the new rulers in 1664 who put an end to the wars) — is still held in the Ulster Co. Archive at Kingston, where I had to make a special appointment to see it. The idea of reconciliation occurred to me then.

In Darjeeling, India, 1970, as part of my initiation in Tara Tantra I was empowered to make offerings to Mars; so at 1:30 PM on Tuesday (sacred to Mars) July 13, which happens to be a "Corn" Day in the Mayan calendar, Charles Stein and I rendevous'd with Rachel Pollack, and Shiv and James from Woodstock, at the Kingston Plaza Pizzeria, which happens to have a rear exit opening directly onto the Dyke. I showed & told about the offerings, which were contained in a druidic "Crane Bag," i.e. a brown paper grocery sack sealed with repeated rows of my Crane seal and my Thoth/Ibis seal:

(Note: Cranes are heraldic for me because of my Scots ancestors the Cranstons — see Scott's "Lay of the Last Minstrel" — and cranes are also sacred to druids and Chinese Immortals; the Egyptian crane, the ibis, is the animal form of Thoth/Hermes.)

We then walked to the tree-lined dirt berm which adjoins the Dyke and climbed down to the River, near what appeared to be a sewage outlet. I hurled the bag into the water, but it landed on a shallow bank; Shiv waded out and pushed it into the deep of the stream, where it sank slowly in a burst of bubbles. This act, according to a nearby sign, constituted an illegal offense, "dumping." James, who had earlier *by chance* purchased some local fresh peaches, threw one of them in, and it floated off downstream. We then retired to El Danzante, a great Mexican restaurant on Broadway in Kingston [now defunct], for a sober but celebratory supper.

(This action was also done in loving memory of Tuli Kupferberg, who died on July 12.)

The Lighthouse at Saugerties
(Photograph by Dennis Willard)

Canto VII/1
The Lighthouse at Saugerties

i. *Dr Brink's Black Bottle Seven Planet Elixir*

recipe for the illegal version
                     revealed to me by his spirit
Sun — calamus root
Moon — poppy (dry pods)
Mercury — ginseng
Venus — applejack
Mars — wormwood
Jupiter — nutmeg
Saturn — hemp
macerate all dry ingredients
cover w/ applejack
let it sit (in a corked bottle) for 7 weeks
stir occasionally
strain
add molasses for color (black) & taste
sweet to mask the bitter herbs

Each Canto of *Esopus — An Epyllion* appears under its own planetary signs, viz.:
1. Lake Winnisook to Phoenicia — Mercury
2. Oscar Wilde in the Catskills — Moon
3. Allegory of the Esopus — Jupiter & Venus
4. Swimming Holes — Moon
5. Dr Brink & the Witches — Sun & Moon
6. Esopus Wars — Mars
7. Lighthouse at Saugerties — Saturn

    The actions at each site are sealed w/ planetary seals acc. to Agrippa & Solomon's Key, etc., w/appropriate incense; consult *6th & 7th Books of Moses, The Long Hidden Friend, Le Pullet Noir.* The culmination at Saugerties Lighthouse should involve a major conjuration & Hermetic Pic-nic of Seven Planets &/or Four Elements
    Dr Brink's cordial served to chosen guests

modelled on the Banquet served to Poliphilo
by Queen "Freedom" in the *Hypnerotomachia* (see below)
using local Hudson Valley produce but also
rare spices drugs condiments wines & gold leaf
Saturn — indigo — shiny lead
Jupiter — citrine (pale clear yellow) or sky blue
Mars — fire red
Sun — glittering orange (or gold)
Venus — shining white
Mercury — green
Moon — silver

The Saugerties Lighthouse in Winter

ii. Lighthouse Riff

The Anti-Jehovah's Witness LIGHTHOUSE
Pharos = phallus = cigar
Cyclops lies on his couch smoking a Monte Cristo
60 feet high while stroking his Herculean club
Popeye in the *Tijuana Bible* eats spinach
unleashes a lingam thick and long as his forearm
pronging out the universe like onanist Egyptian god
alone in an infinite swamp of conjecture
whole world a vast masturbation fantasy
alone in a lighthouse
                  yet mysteriously pregnant
primordial Madam Adam
    in top hat & lace gown
        reveals all for
               25¢
lover beloved love all one
          as the sufis never
              tire of repeating
in their monotonous guttural
    hypnotic trance-inducing chanting
              in the ears of
Gérard de Nerval
        & the whole French Irrationalist Left
        (Gide — Foucault — Genet — those
        paederastic muslimophiles)
to the music of an *'oud* that leads
          down the garden path
into sexual frustration so extreme
    it often proves fatal as
        autocombustion
            martyrs to chaste desire
            guaranteed entry to that
            fleshly heaven of the
              saracens.
Lighthouse as Bachelardian poetic space

round as the moon-tower in
                    Dream of the Red Chamber
round as the round towers of
                    Ireland or Ilium
truncated cone or obeliskoid lighthouse
theorem of light ray in its very shape
architecture that is what it does &
                              means what it is
Goldilock's Tower: Stella Maris. O
that Neptunian funk — you can smell it
     all the way to the whaling port of Hudson
or even Albany — cormorants gulls seabirds
                                   follow the lunar
                                           sigh

Welcome to Vinland (Ruskin said it:
                    the light of a countryside
                    where grapes grow is a
                    superior light) —
                              the Nordic Atlantis
the NorthWest Passage our brackish fjord
                    our river of light
                              above the river
                                   of water —
our *atmosphere.*

The lighthouse is a pure Ahuramazdian
guaranteed good thing
               casts not shadows but light
               plus you can actually live inside
be the mental phosphorus in its crystal
carbuncle of maritime hallelullias
utterly aloof aloft above all mere human
malignant buffoonery &
                    police surveillance.
And marry a mermaid one fine night.
And nibelungize the Hudsonian biosphere
w/ imported
               Rhenish castles of
                    re-inforced concrete
& pseudo-Ottoman octagons
               of Rosendale cement.
A Machine for Reverie. For
               scanning horizons w/ spyglass
               like Buster Keaton as Galileo
in the Existentialist melody

sad yet defiant
of a Stirnerite Individualist
w/ a ukelele —
clear night
stars reflected in the river's slack
slick tide —
as above so below.

Balor's Tower
Balor of the one big Evil Eye
Fomorian giant lizard blacksmith
of Tory Island.
Cornish wreckers. Rum smugglers
need a dark light to land their contraband
to wade ashore w/ kegs of brandy
laudanum & ambergris
on moony nights as
cut-rate Captain Kidds
lighthouse the candle in a
Hand of Glory
lighthouse will-o-the-wisp torch in a swamp
in the trembling hand of some treasure-seeking sucker
for the cheap grimoires of Upstate rodomancers*
Black lighthouse of Anarchy & obsidian onyx
land of Sleep's
green marble silent halls &
columns of polluted jet
lighthouse of necromancy
— Obeah — Petro —
Hoodoo Yezidi Peacock Angel
ebony cane of Baron Saturday
w/ its luminous knob —
the religion of get
what you want
money power sex & gourmet food.
Get what you want
before you have to die
shad roe champagne attar
of cock's crow
electric eel & poison blowfish sushi —
trembling smoke.

---

* One who seeks buried treasure with a magic *rod* or wand. Very popular in early 19th-century New York state.

Beacon of Julian
the Apostate the
Egyptian Magical Papyri
torch of Hekate
lamp of heresy — blow it out
& in the darkness weep.

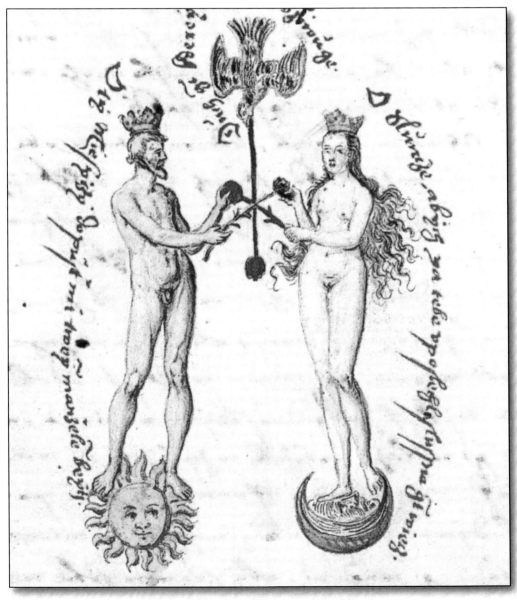

Thomas Vaughn's "Alchemical Wedding"

iii. Euphrates

(for Thomas Vaughan, Alchemist & Rosicrucian)

This is not mere selfishness on my part — in fact it's sheer altruism that forces me to
keep certain secrets in order to persuade you (O daughter of Hermes) in a moment of
metanoia that
    secrets
        still
            exist
venery means the hunt
venery means the art of love
veneration means one-pointed attentiveness
Ignatz & Krazy Kat, not the tourist, the
pilgrim not consumer of images who
never gives anything back to the land
                                      except money
who sucks away picturesque sublime holy till nothing's left
                but dry bones
Hermetic Art conceals to force the Reader/Seer to read/see presence
behind representation
veils itself in obscene cartoons &
                    re-arranges the furniture
enter the labyrinth
                really get lost
weasel yr way out w/ cunning & cheating
the Map is Not the Territory
                    — & yet it is —
                        map of geomantic gestures
occult hydrochorography or -choreography of the
sole en-soul'd universe.

On the plus side:
                geologic shapes & slants of sunlight
stamped into silvered icons by
                    Freddy the Pig Detective

who came from nearby Roxbury (Delaware Co.)
up there in Anti-Rent country
                          near West Bovina
beyond the scope of this present poem
a Gog-Magog giant the size of the whole mythosphere
murmuring & tossing in geo-psychic sleep
a vast Arthurian figure seen dimly as yet
but sooner or later he'll get up.

Ice Yachts

iv. The Bishop of Galatia

today is our captain
of this ice yacht from Barrytown
looming skeletal wooden gull ice-skate
                                        white spinnaker
   — up to 60 mph — the luddite world record
so fast it hangs in the air like
                        Nijinski as swan
still-standing *en jeté* while
the River seems to scroll backwards at
                  breakneck racehorse speed
in slash of rhinestones leaving behind it a
                  wake of crushed & wasted cocaine
azure oxygen & bitter
                        sunlight — — behind him
purple dalmatic & cope streaming
                        flutter'd ribbands
one hand on mitre the other waving a crazy crozier
only organic speed is real speed
the body understands it
wind can out-race gasoline
jaguar's faster than rocketship
                  flower quicker than seed

The See of Galatia established by St Paul & treated to his famous scolding letter
arose from Celtic invasion of Asia Minor 3rd century BC by Gaels or Gauls on their way
from Scythia to Greece, then others went to Egypt where Scota daughter of Pharaoh
married Mil, King of the Milesian Celts, & invaded Ireland from Spain — she's buried
under a dolmen in Co. Kerry — What DNA would unveil the forgotten Galatians who
once ruled Ancyra Bithynia Anatolia all the way to the Sea.

Were the Celts expelled?

No.

Were they exterminated by the Ottomans?

No.

Ergo they're still there — druid mysteries survive in heretical sects sufi orders &
crypto-Xtians such as Bektashis, wine-drinkers,
    antinomians who eventually infiltrated Ottoman Grand-Orient
FreeMasonry
        which granted Charters to American Black Shriners at the 1893 Chicago
World's Fair, who passed them on to
        the Moorish Science
Temple in Newark NJ in 1913,
        were also infiltrated by followers of the False Messiah
Sabbatai Sevi in Salonika — Rudolf von Sebbottendorf, spymaster of Ariosophy & the
Thulegesellschaft who executed a number of anarchists at the Four Seasons Hotel in Mu-
nich, May 1918, claimed to have penetrated Ottoman Masonry, & was assassinated on a
bridge in Istanbul on the last day of WW II.

    The Bishop of Galatia is of course
        Exilarch as well as Logothete
            of the Byzantine Empire
   involved in his youth with
        IRA splinter groups
         & Col. Qaddafi

   most of the Wandering Bishops were queer — an Old Catholic Church Home for
Wayward Boys busted in London in the 1950s — Bishop Leadbeater had to leave Aus-
tralia in disarray — our own Archbishop Michael Itkin used to attend Greenwich Village
gay-lib demo's in full ecclesiastical regalia — on roller skates — waving sexual revolution
placards & blessing the mob.

   The Bishop of Galatia
        drinks deep in an Irish bar
           in Poughkeepsie
weeps over rebel songs in his cups
of baby Powers & halfpint of Murphy's
He summers in the Irish Catskills
around E. Durham in Greene Co. where he
gives seminars on Yeats   AE   the Celtic Twilight
James Clarence Mangan the Irish Poe
Druid Freemasonry & the American Revolution
Ireland's Links with Moorish & Turkish Culture
badly attended at some thirdrate
integral holistic weekend yoga spa
   crumbling former Jewish Commie Summer Camp

dismal failure as Newage Xtian guru
too besotted unkempt & sarcastic
now the Bishop is reduced to
working as Janitor for poor but very High
Episcopal church known as Smoky Mary's in
                              shabby neighborhood
behind Poughkeepsie Railway Station
(which station happens to be
the center of the Universe)
sad room in the basement, a.k.a. "crypt"
under the title Sacristan & Verger
w/ zero salary & psychotropic overdoses
                         of frankincense
living on pitiful remittance from family in Izmir or Dublin
reading Jacob Boehme in bed or
                  haunting public pool at YMCA
to see those flashes of pewter light
that induce epiphany
an old sufi practice
         in Turkish bathhouses

But suddenly
money arrives from unknown agency
money the Bishop declares "free" & hence purely hermetic
joyfully decides to waste it in realizing one
      rare & exquisite ambition
he rents Saugerties Lighthouse (at confluence of Esopus
                                 & the Hudson)
for a weekend in February when it's accessible only
                              by ice-yacht
invites a handful of friends gourmet artists & Famous Beauties
a lutenist & a chef to an Ice Fest w/ all-day all-nite
Pansophic Hermetic Feast of the Seven Planets
& Four Elements plus rare vintages
                  & alchemic distillates
viva voce reading of ESOPUS: A Choromantric Epyllion
His Reverence the Bishop & Metropolitan of Galatia
interspersed w/ spins on the ice
                         to whet appetites
for gastrosophist gesamtkunstwerk of the Twelve Senses
                         surrounded by ICE.
And this was the Menu:

In the presence of the magnificent Queen, there were always three demure maidens
at her service, furnished with overgarments of gold marvellously woven with silk. These

delighted the eye by changing their colours along with the changing of the table-cloths, such that when they changed the cloths, the servants also changed their nymphal garments to the corresponding colour. An elegant swatch of material emerged from their tight belts to circle around the snow-white flesh of their shoulders and over their generous bosoms, which swelled moderately beneath it, revealing the valley of their breasts: it was so extremely voluptuous as to make the richest food seem meagre to the spectators. These costumes were luxuriously decorated with a thousand coils and cords of gold and silk, destined with feminine wiles to provoke the pleasure of free and amorous glances, sweet and delectable to a degree beyond that of any favoured and delicious dish. They wore shoes of gold with a moon-shaped opening above the naked foot, all voluptuously secured in the same way with golden clasps. Their abundant blond hair flowed down as far as their calves, and was encircled above their white brows with strings of great matching pearls. These three served before the Queen with especial devotion and reverence, very adroit in their performance of this duty and exceptionally prompt in its execution, serving none but this one table. At each changing of the tables, they all stayed standing after their service was done, with their arms folded in reverent fashion; and thus did all the others who succeeded them, always remaining the same in number.

Of the three servants ministering to each guest, the one in the middle presented the food, the one on the right interposed a plate beneath the food so that nothing should fall, and the third, on the left, elegantly wiped the guest's lips with a white napkin, soft and perfectly clean. After each action they promply curtsied. The napkin was not reused in this service: the maiden dropped it on the pavement, whence it was promptly collected and taken away; and as many napkins were brought as there were morsels to be served. They were fragrantly scented, folded, and wonderfully woven from silk.

This table service was observed diligently for each of the guests, so that no one touched any of the food, but was fed at will by the servant except for the cup.

After the first course, everyone washed in the ingenious fountain that I have described, in which the fallen water was raised again by the force of the air that was received or enclosed. I pondered on this exquisite device, and was extremely gratified to realize, after careful investigation, that the vase was divided inside by means of two pipes of unequal bore, with an inserted plate perforated in the middle, and that the water was forced to ascend by its own impulse.

After everyone had washed, first the Queen and then all the rest, the refined serving maidens gave to each a pear-shaped pomander of gold, finely pierced and containing a mixed paste of marvellous fragrance, so that their idle hands should be busied with something, and the senses of sight and smell delighted with this ball or toy, with its decorations of precious stones.

Then, at every change of course, two beautiful table servants pulled into the middle of the royal court a stupendous buffet on four rolling wheels, with its front made in the form of a boat or drinking cup and the back shaped like a triumphal chariot. It was made of pure gold, decorated with many scyllas and little sea monsters and a host of other exquisite images miraculously worked, and wonderfully ornamented all over with precious stones in elegant arrangements. These scintillated so as to light the whole surrounding area, and their blaze met in every direction with the flashing of other jewels in various places, so that one might well have said that Phoebus was here with his radiant hair. There was a nymph sitting on it, whose face was no less fair than her bright eyes. One could add nothing, nor even find anything to equal the continuous lustre and splendour of these ineffable artefacts — not even the Temple of Babylon with its three golden statues.

The interior of the chariot was well stocked with all manner of condiments and sauces, suiting the needs of every kind of table. It contained tablecloths, flowers, cups, napkins, vases, forks, drinks, food and seasonings. This charioteer nymph prepared them and promptly handed them out for distribution.

When the tables were taken down for the change of course, everything on them, as described above, was returned to the buffet-chariot. This then departed, and the maidens immediately began to sound their curved trumpets — such as were never invented by Pisaeus, son of Tyrrhenus, nor by Maletus, king of Etruria — and the flautists played with them. Thus it was done each time the buffet went out: they played until it returned and then stopped. Whenever the tables were changed, the musical instruments did like-

wise; and when they ceased, the singers began in the Aeolian mode, so sweetly as to make the Sirens sigh, accompanied by reed pipes and double flutes such as Troezenius Dardanus never invented. In this way one was always hearing lovely music, listening to gentle harmonies, harkening to delectable melodies, breathing delightful perfumes and receiving the most delicious satisfaction of the appetite. Everything came together faultlessly for the sake of dignity, grace and pleasure.

All the utensils or instruments at this supreme and splendid table were of fine gold, as was the round table in front of the Queen. Now a

cordial confection was presented, which I think I am right in saying was a healthy compound made mostly of powdered unicorn's horn, the two kinds of sandalwood, ground pearls in brandy set alight so as to dissolve them completely, manna, pine-nuts, rosewater, musk and powdered gold: a very precious mixture, weighed and pressed out in morsels with fine sugar and starch. We were given two servings of this, at a moderate interval and without drinking in between. It is food for preventing every harmful fever and for dispelling all sorrowful fatigue.

After this, everything was taken away in an instant: the fragrant violets were scattered on the ground and the table was stripped. No sooner was this done than the table was covered once more with a sea-coloured cloth, and all the servants were wearing the same. Then, as before, they covered it with fragrant flowers of citrine, orange and lemon, and then presented in vases of beryl (and the Queen's table was of the same stone, except for the forks, which were of gold) five cakes or fritters made from saffron-coloured dough with hot rosewater and sugar, coiled and finely sprinkled with the same musk-flavoured water and with powdered sugar. These globes were delicious to the taste and very various, having been carefully cooked in the following ways: the first one offered was in olive-flower oil; the second, in clove oil; the last, in oil pressed from musk and amber. After we had tasted this delectable dainty and savoured it with avid and keen appetite, we were presented with a solemn cup made, together with its cover, from the stone already mentioned. There was also a fine silken veil covering it, embroidered in vermiculate work with silk and gold, which was then thrown over the shoulder of the bearer and hung down her back. All the drinking and eating vessels were covered and presented in this fashion. This chalice was filled with a precious wine: I suspected without a doubt that the god who makes the vintage in the Elysian Fields had infused this sweet liquid with his divinity, for it was unrivalled by Thasian wine or by any other precious liquor.

After this welcome drink, the table was taken down without delay, and the fragrant flowers strewn on the shiny pavement. A tablecloth of purple silk was quickly laid, and a mixture of roses scattered on it: incarnadine or mallow, white, vermilion, musk, Damascus, four-leaved and Jebbedine. The new servants, dressed in

the same cloth and colour, nimbly brought to each guest six cuts of fattened, blinded capon, moistened with its own fat, sprinkled with yellow rosewater mixed with orange juice, roasted to perfection and then gilded all over. With this came six slices of snow-white bridal bread, and beside it a sauce of lemon ice modified with fine sugar mashed with pine nuts and the capon's liver, to which were added rosewater, musk, saffron and choice cinnamon; and all these flavourings were compounded in special and exquisite proportion, and perfectly seasoned. All the dishes were made from topaz, and so was the round tabletop.

This third frugal and magnificent table was dismantled like the others, then without delay it was newly covered with a satin cloth of bright yellow (and the servants clothed in the same), and all flowered over with fragrant lilies-of-the-valley and narcissus. The food was straightaway presented: seven pieces of partridge meat, roasted diligently at the fire, and as many mouthfuls of yeasty milk bread. The sauce was sharp, with crushed almonds, thrice cooked sugar, starch, yellow sandalwood, musk and rosewater; the dishes were of chrysolith, as was the circular table. At the end they proffered the precious chalice, and so it was done in the succeeding courses.

When this fourth rich course was removed, the table was relaid for the fifth with a crimson silk cloth, and the nymphs clothed in the same. The flowers were yellow, white, and amethystine Cairo roses; the food consisted of eight morsels of choicest, succulent roast pheasant meat, and as many pieces of a light white bread. The sauce was thus: fresh egg yolks with pine nuts, orange water, pomegranate juice, Colossine sugar and cinnamon. The dishes were of emerald, and so was the table of the sublime Queen.

After this solemn course was cleared, there was no delay before spreading a cloth of violet silk, with matching garments for the nymphs. The flowers were the three kinds of jasmine: red, yellow and white. The food was nine mouthfuls of long-lasting peacock's

breast, roasted in its juices, fat and well grilled. There was a sour green sauce with ground pistachio nuts, Cyrian sugar, starch, musk, wild thyme, white oregano and pepper. The dishes and the royal table were of blue sapphire.

After this sixth rich course, they brought in a sumptuous table all made from white ivory subtly pieced together, in which was set another one of precious aloe wood, well compacted with glue and engraved from one end to the other with a wonderful design of noble knotwork, with foliage, flowers, vases, little monsters and birds, filled in with a black compound made from musk and amber. I reckoned this, with good reason, to be a most elegant and luxurious thing, with an odour that was delightful to breathe. The cloth was fine and white, with vermiculate embroidery of Carystian cotton, the same cloth as was worn by the serving maidens. The flowers were cyclamens together with every kind of carnation, excessively fragrant: I dare not express the delight to the senses caused by such sweet and varied scents in ever new combinations. The excellent confection was morsels made from date-pulp and pistachios ground with rosewater, sugar of the Isles and musk, mixed with precious powdered gold so that the entire thing seemed to be made of gold. Three of these were given to each. The dishes and the circular table were of hyacinth, a suitable stone for the excellent setting of the divine and magnificent table, and not subject to Licinia's sumptuary laws.

Thanks to Jocelyn Godwin, translator of the *Hypnerotomachia*, publ. by Thames & Hudson.